14.07.92

Dear Gwen:

While reading this I thought of a picture of you in uniform during W.W. II, of Howard and of a poem you wrote early, as I remember, in the war.

I can't now remember anything of the poem except that its end rhymes were true, and that its spirit had an élan I liked.

Sincerely, John.

WE STAND ON GUARD

POEMS AND SONGS OF CANADIANS
IN BATTLE

COMPILED BY
JOHN ROBERT COLOMBO
AND MICHAEL RICHARDSON

FOREWORD BY
RICHARD ROHMER

Library of Congress Catalog Card Number: 85-15996
This edition text copyright © 1985 by John Robert Colombo and
Michael Richardson
Foreword copyright © by Richard Rohmer
All rights reserved
First edition
Interior design by Don Fernley
Typesetting by Compeer Typographic Services Limited
Printed and bound in Canada by John Deyell Company
Cover photo courtesy Patricia Giesler.

Canadian Cataloguing in Publication Data

Main entry under title:
  We stand on guard

ISBN 0-385-25002-9

1. War poetry — Canada.   2. War-songs — Canada.
I. Colombo, John Robert, 1936–   II. Richardson, Michael, 1946–

PS8287.W37W42 1985   C811′.008′0358   C85-099441-1
PR9195.85.W37W42 1985

THIS BOOK IS DEDICATED
TO THE CANADIANS
WHO FOUGHT AND DIED FOR FREEDOM

CONTENTS

13. THE SPANISH CIVIL WAR *128*

14. THE SECOND WORLD WAR *133*

FOREWORD

Canadians at war? For two generations of Canadians this is a most difficult concept to grasp. The reason is very simple. Canada — except for a limited foray in the Korean War at the beginning of the fifties — has not had a war to fight since 1945. The nation has not had to call upon its youth to take up arms and to sacrifice lives and suffer lifelong injuries, for four decades. These decades have been a time of peace, if not tranquility, during which the battles of World War I and World War II have receded into the memories of the people involved — some 11 million during World War II, far fewer during World War I. Those memories do not exist at all for the generations that have followed and for the masses that have come to Canada since 1945 to swell its population to over 24 million. Except in wartime when the nation has been galvanized to perform spectacular feats of arms, bravery, and industrial accomplishments in the building of ships and aircraft and all manner of armaments, the perception, knowledge, and understanding of the Canadian military, both past and present, has diminished in the public and political eye.

The fact is that in peacetime Canada is not a militaristic nation. It does not carry the burden of leading the world against the communist threat, and indeed, it looks to the American people to the south to defend its territory and its freedom. Since World War II, the Canadian people have become nonmilitaristic but not quite yet pacifist. Indeed, we view ourselves as a people friendly with all nations. Certainly we have maintained some degree of partnership in our contribution to the North Atlantic Treaty Organization, and we have provided men for United Nations peacekeeping forces in the Middle East and Cyprus. International peacekeeping has been one of the cornerstones of our foreign policy.

In times of peace, Canadians are inclined to overlook the importance of their soldiers, sailors, and airmen, whether full time or reservists. Be that as it may, the Canadian military, on land and sea and in the air, has played a significant part in the growth and development, and indeed, in the establishment of the Canadian nation. The songs and poems that have been evoked by our battles, the victories and the losses, are songs of glory, victory, and exultation. The words and thoughts are inspiring, born in the minds and hearts of Canadians who have fought and died and suffered in battle, believing that their sacrifices were for the good of the nation, for the cause of everlasting peace.

A collection of the songs, poems, and verses produced by Canadians in time of war and battle is long overdue. The moving and compelling lyrics and sentiments that will be found in this book will provide new insights into the emotions and psychologies of the Canadians who participated in the War of 1812, the Battle of Batoche, the Boer War, the world wars, and other significant military clashes in which Canada has taken part. This collection will convey to the reader some of the human energy, self-sacrifice, and even at times wrong-headedness that characterizes Canada's people "standing on guard" in past days. It provides unique insights into the minds of people long dead who helped shape this magnificent country and make it what it is today—the finest place in the world in which to live.

RICHARD ROHMER
Major General (retired)

ACKNOWLEDGEMENTS

The editors are grateful to a great many people who assisted in the compilation of this anthology. Research was conducted at the Metropolitan Toronto Library and the North York Public Library, where the librarians and staff were most helpful. Special thanks at Metro Central are owed to Cameron Hollyer, Mary Anne Tessaro, and David Kotin; and at North York to Pat Jenkins, Margaret Hortopan, and Irena Bernas of the Canadiana Collection and James Pendergest of Bathurst Heights. Philip Singer assisted in many ways.

We are pleased that Richard Rohmer agreed to contribute the foreword. Major General Rohmer served as a fighter-reconnaissance pilot with the RCAF and was awarded the Distinguished Flying Cross in 1945. He was appointed Chief of Reserves of the Canadian Armed Forces in 1979, retiring from the post in 1981. He is, of course, one of the country's most widely read novelists, an early proponent of the Mid-Canada Corridor concept, and no mean military historian.

We are pleased, as well, to acknowledge assistance received from W. A. B. Douglas, director, Directorate of History, National Defence Headquarters, Ottawa.

Legion, the official magazine of the Royal Canadian Legion, carried our request for remembered war songs and ditties in its July 1984 issue. We wish to thank its editor, Jane Dewar, for bringing our project to the attention of the *Legion*'s readers. Some sixty veterans responded to our request and sent us more than two hundred verses. We would like to acknowledge all the readers by name but will have to limit ourselves to a handful: Phylis Bowman, Prince Rupert, British Columbia; Carl Collens, Stouffville, Ontario; Daisy

Cook, Regina, Saskatchewan; George Dann, London, Ontario; W. D. Ellis, Toronto, Ontario; Strome Galloway, Ottawa, Ontario; R. E. Henley, Brentwood Bay, British Columbia; J. Stuart McClean, London, Ontario; Jane Morgan, Thornton, Ontario; Norman Mycock, Victoria, British Columbia; Gregory A. Oakes, Elora, Ontario; W. Ray Stephens, Oakville, Ontario; Tommy Thomson, Victoria, British Columbia; F. B. Watt, Toronto, Ontario. Mr. Stephens was of considerable assistance with the songs of the period.

Many other men and women, veterans and literary people alike, came to our aid. They include the following: Edmund C. Bovey, The Canadian Naval Corvette Trust, Toronto, Ontario; Jack Bush, Toronto, Ontario; Patrick Crean, Toronto, Ontario; Louis Dudek, Montreal, Quebec; Win and Gordon Ely, Toronto, Ontario; Edith Fowke, Toronto, Ontario; J. L. (Jack) Granatstein, Toronto, Ontario. Michael Richardson would like to acknowledge the insights on war given him by Joseph, Bob, Harry, and Tommy Bartlett, Geoff Dykes, and his father, the late Norman Ralph Richardson.

We Stand on Guard may be the first comprehensive collection of its type, but there were notable, albeit circumscribed, collections of war songs and poems published in the past. The present editors are indebted to past editors who compiled their anthologies, largely in times of war, for patriotic purposes. Here are the details about earlier publications every student of soldiers' songs and poetry should study: John D. Borthwich, *Poems and Songs of the South African War* (1901); Canadian Authors Association's *Voices of Victory: Representative Poetry of Canada in War-Time* (1941); George Herbert Clarke, *A Treasury of War Poetry* (first series 1917; second series 1919), *A New Treasury of War Poetry* (1943); N. Brian Davies, *The Poetry of the Canadian People* (volume 1, 1976; volume 2, 1978); Edith Fowke, with Alan Mills, *Singing Our History: Canada's Story in Song* (1984); John W. Garvin, *Canadian Poems of the Great War* (1918); Anthony Hopkins, *Songs from the Front and Rear: Canadian Servicemen's Songs of the Second World War* (1979); W. D. Lighthall, *Songs of the Great Dominion* (1889), *Canadian Poets of the Great War* (1916); John S. Moir, *Rhymes of Rebellion* (1965); Charles G. D. Roberts, *Flying Colours* (1942).

In addition to these anthologies, some collections and studies were of signal significance, notably: Margaret Fairley's *The Spirit of Canadian Democracy* (1945); Carl F. Klinck and R. E. Watters's *Checklist of Canadian Literature* (1959); Heather Robertson's *A Terrible Beauty: The Art of Canada at War* (1977); Norah Story's *The Oxford Companion to Canadian History and Literature* (1967); Herbert Fairlie Wood and John Swettenham's *Silent Witness* (1974). Two non-Canadian books that raised relevant questions are Paul Fussell's *The Great War and Modern Memory* (1975) and Denis Winter's *Death's Men: Soldiers of the Great War* (1978).

We wish to thank Denise Schon and John Neale, of Doubleday Canada Limited, for their interest in this project.

Our principal indebtedness is to the men and women of all the Canadian campaigns, especially those who made the supreme sacrifice. This indebtedness was brought home to one of the editors by the pupils of Church Street Public School, Toronto. They staged their annual Christmas concert in December 1984 and called it "Peace on Earth." The schoolchildren answered the question why the soldier-poets fought and wrote: To live in peace.

O CANADA

O Canada! Our home and native land!
True patriot love in all thy sons command!
With glowing hearts we see thee rise,
The True North strong and free!
From far and wide, O Canada,
We stand on guard for thee.
God keep our land glorious and free!
O Canada, we stand on guard for thee.
O Canada, we stand on guard for thee.

O Canada! Terre de nos aïeux,
Ton front est ceint de fleurons glorieux!
Car ton bras sait porter l'épée,
Il sait porter la croix!
Ton histoire est une épopée
Des plus brillants exploits.
Et ta valeur, de foi trempée,
Protégera nos foyers et nos droits.
Protégera nos foyers et nos droits.

The words and the music of "O Canada" were declared the National Anthem of Canada—*Hymne national du Canada* by An Act Respecting the National Anthem of Canada, which received Royal Assent on June 27, 1980, and was proclaimed on July 1, 1980.

INTRODUCTION

We Stand on Guard is the first comprehensive collection of songs, poems, and verses of Canadians in battle. It brings together approximately one hundred and fifty compositions by known and unknown composers, poets, and versifiers. Their compositions come from commercially published, privately printed, and unpublished manuscript sources. Over the years other editors have collected songs and poems connected with specific expeditions, campaigns, rebellions, and wars; but until now no one has attempted to represent, in a variety of poetic forms in the pages of a single book, three centuries of Canadian martial experience.

Here are some of the songs Canadian soldiers sang. Here are some of the poems Canadian soldiers wrote. Here are some of the verses Canadian soldiers recited. Here are, as well, compositions written by other Canadians, distant from fields of battle, about the dedication and daring of Canadian soldiers. (The word "Canada" has been extended in time to include the land long before it became a country, and the word "soldiers" has been taken to embrace Indian warriors.) Indeed, the anthology begins with Indian Battles, and ends with Future Battles. In between there are engagements enjoined by native warriors, armed *habitants* and *voyageurs*, volunteers, members of the militia, British regulars, the Mounted Police, the Canadian Expeditionary Force, the Canadian Corps, members of the Army, Navy, Air Force, and now of the Canadian Armed Forces. They fought valiantly and well, and many died on fields of battle at home and abroad.

1

Some characteristics of the present collection require discussion. Unlike previous anthologies, the present one presents songs and poems side by side. The editors hold that the differences between verses of a song and stanzas of a poem when they appear on the printed page are negligible, especially when they have so much in common and the *subject* is most relevant. The earliest battles are remembered, when they are recalled at all, through their songs. The more recent engagements are celebrated more often than not through poetry and protested in song. So in this anthology both forms of lyrical utterance are present.

Another characteristic of the present collection is that it brings together compositions that are both contemporaneous with the events described and contemporary with the reader today. The military engagements follow one another chronologically, within sections, but within each section the reader may expect to encounter a traditional folk song cheek-by-jowl with a contemporary poem. Historical and modern points of view are thus brought into relief.

Yet another characteristic is that some of the compositions were written by participants, others by observers. In truth, the genuine soldier-poet, like Lieutenant Colonel John McCrae, was a rare bird. Many soldiers wrote poems and verses, but few were genuine poets or even competent versifiers. The compositions that endure were largely written by recognized writers with military experience. One thinks of the war poetry of Raymond Souster, Douglas LePan, George Whalley, and Bertram Warr to realize how rare is literary talent among enlisted — and civilian — men and women.

No bibliography of Canadian war poetry and song has ever been prepared, so when the editors began their task they were working in the dark. In order to make the best selection from available texts (largely published but including some unpublished material), they examined more than two hundred separate publications, ranging from regimental song books to volumes of verse and anthologies of poetry. They also looked at one hundred pieces of sheet music issued over imprints like Gordon V. Thompson, and solicited original and oral compositions. Limiting the selection to separate book-length publications, one may assume that each of the two hundred publications offered the reader at least fifty compositions, so there were approximately ten thousand compositions. In addition, much fugitive material in old newspapers and magazines was examined. The material was abundant.

But what about quality? The editors early on came to the conclusion that literary quality, although a consideration in the selection process, was not the prime concern. How else could they reconcile representing such a variety of modes and interests—songs as boisterous as "Mademoiselle from Armentières" or as elegiac as "Un Canadien Errant," poems as sentimental but moving as "This Was My Brother" by Mona Gould or as accomplished and modernistic as "On Going to the Wars" by Earle Birney? Yet, on balance, they feel that the material is charged with literary interest and that some of the compositions are instances of high art.

Once the editors had familiarized themselves with the material, they had to decide what to exclude. They quickly agreed on seven areas of exclusion to keep the anthology within manageable reading and publishing limits.

First, they generally ignored popular songs that were sentimental favourites on the home front. "The World Is Waiting for the Sunrise" may have given expression to the hope for a better world in 1919, and "I'll Never Smile Again" may have given voice to fears for the future in 1939, and both may be Canadian compositions, but the lyrics of neither are reprinted here.

Second, the editors found little room for songs, poems, or verses that made use of martial occasions for meditations on piety or patriotism. They preferred vivid descriptions of front-line conditions and analyses of psychological states of stress to perfunctory prayers to God, odes to freedom, and quasi-anthems to country. Although the anthology is a collection of military material, noticeably absent from its pages are coy or cloying pietistic, militaristic, or jingoistic statements.

Third, the editors gave short shrift to works that achieved some degree of popularity in their own day and fell by the wayside in our own. This decision required the exclusion of poems of the Canada-to-Britain variety, in which the Dominion assures the Mother Country of undying fealty and the delivery of a contingent of troops. Swept aside was "Langemarck," despite the fact that Wilfred Campbell's lengthy work, written in praise of Lord Kitchener in April

1915, was the first poem telegraphed to newspapers around the world. Stanzas like the following — "This is the battle of Langemarck, / A story of glory and might; / Of the vast Hun horde, and Canada's part / In the great, grim fight" — are not included, for they tell us more about popular taste than they do about war or the human spirit.

Fourth, the editors reprinted only a handful of regimental songs. The official and semi-official marching and other songs of the Canadian regiments are well worth reading, if not singing, but many of them have miles of verses, acres of versions, and deserve volumes of their own. Nonetheless, a few songs associated with the Princess Patricia's Canadian Light Infantry — the redoubtable Princess Pats — are included to give a taste of what is missing.

Fifth, the editors backed away from bawdy verse. This is what most people have in mind when the subject of "war songs" comes up. Some of the lyrics included are suggestive but none are filthy. It would be well worth publishing a collection of bawdy songs sung by Canadian servicemen (and servicewomen), but that is not our concern. Any reader who wishes to peruse the scansion of "North Atlantic Squadron," the most notorious dirty song of Canadian servicemen, will have to turn to the words and music included by Anthony Hopkins in his durable collection, *Songs from the Front and Rear*.

Sixth, the editors regret that there are so few lyrics from French Canada. This slim representation is unavoidable, given the unpopularity in Quebec of the two world wars, works about which constitute the bulk of this collection. (Did not Henri Bourassa declare, "Our first line of defence is at Ottawa"?) As well, poems familiar to Quebeckers are not necessarily known even by name outside the province. Literary compositions suffer in the hands of translators, and there are so few Canadians who have attempted to translate popular French material into English. It is especially regrettable that the patriotic war poetry of Octave Crémazie and Louis-Honoré Fréchette is so little known in English Canada. Such poetry, well translated, would have an honoured place in any English-language anthology.

Seventh, and last, the present selection is principally one of lyrical poetry and song. There is less narrative verse than the editors enjoyed reading. Narratives in verse, whether written in the ballad form or some other style, is invariably lengthy, and space is always at a premium. Much narrative verse displays the excesses of the period of its composition and is quickly dated.

A number of narrative poems are represented through excerpts, yet it may be useful to the reader to see a short list of book-length poems or collections of linked poems about martial experiences, if only to serve as a supplement to the present volume. Here are the names of the authors and their works: Philip Child: *The Wood of the Nightingale*; Robert Finch: *Dover Beach Revisited*; A. M. Klein: *The Hitleriad*; Douglas LePan: *The Net and the Sword*; Dorothy Livesay: *Call My People Home, Catalonia, Prophet of the New World*; Douglas Lochhead: Ted Plantos: *Passchendaele*; E. J. Pratt: *Dunkirk, Behind the Log*; Raymond Souster: *Jubilee of Death, Pictures From a Long Lost World*; Joseph Schull: *I, Jones, Soldier*; Duncan Campbell Scott: *The Battle of Lundy's Lane*; Peter Taylor: *Trainer*; David West: *Trenchmist*; George Whalley: *No Man An Island*.

The reader might wonder, with all these exclusions, what is left. What remains is a parade of songs, poems, and verses that re-create for the contemporary reader the sights and sounds, sensations and feelings, ideals and deals, of Canada's fighting men and women. Over the centuries, and especially the three centuries the present anthology surveys, the nature of warfare has changed. And so has man's way of describing war.

The earliest lyric in this collection is a traditional Iroquois war song, which was translated into English verse in the early nineteenth century. Even in the stilted English of the translator, Henry Rowe Schoolcraft, it takes the reader into the heart and soul of the native warrior. The first singer of this song may have died centuries ago, and he may have died in battle, but no one will ever know, for the work is a traditional one. But it is an Iroquois song, and the Iroquois warriors were the most feared of braves. It expresses for the contemporary reader, as perhaps no other song or poem does in this anthology, the need to die heroically — on the enemy's side of the line.

The poems of the Europeans, which follow the burning intensity of the Iroquois war song, pale in comparison. Whatever their other merits, they mark a point of entry into history. Historians are still debating the importance of the heroism of Adam Dollard and Madeleine Verchères, but there is little debate about the effect that knowledge of their deeds has had on subsequent generations. Adam and Madeleine have become symbols of stiff-necked resistance against all odds. They are popular heroes in French Canada. The section on Indian Battles concludes with Duncan Campbell Scott's portrait of an aged female Indian warrior, as unexpected as it is magnificently dramatic.

The variety of poetic forms included in this collection is nowhere better displayed than in the section on the English and the French. Traditional songs of unknown authorship in both languages, a verse narrative about an event in the distant past, and a poem written within the last decade comprise the section. These are compositions to be sung, recited, or spoken.

The same contrast is to be found in the sections on the American Invasion and the War of 1812. In the latter section there is a sharp contrast between two views of the engagement on Queenston Heights — the traditional one cast in the heroic mould, and the contemporary one cast in the ironic mould. While the Massacre of Seven Oaks may not rank very high in the military annals of the country, here it acts as a showcase for James Reaney's ebullient translation of the best-known ballad of Pierre Falcon, the Métis bard.

The Rebellion of 1837 inspired an immense amount of mediocre rhyme and metre and a miniscule amount of dramatic or lyrical poetry and song. Among the latter is an emotional song about life in exile, "Avant tout je suis Canadien," which is sung in Quebec to this day. The rebellions in Lower and Upper Canada continue to inspire poets, as witness Raymond Souster's graceful elegy for two rebels who were hanged for high treason.

The raids of the Fenians may seem an Irish-American folly these days, but the piece of verbal invective called "The Fenian Blood-Hounds" gives us some sense of how the invaders were feared and detested. And no book about Canada's fighting men and women would be complete without a salute to the Royal Canadian Mounted Police. The famous force may be on parade rather than engaged in battle in "The Riders of the Plains," but it was the presence of

Mounted Police in the Northwest that saved much Canadian blood from being shed.

Order in the Northwest was upset by the Red River Rebellion and the North West Rebellion, the two prairie insurrections led by Louis Riel. The first rebellion, as far as the present editors can determine, inspired no memorable ballads or songs, but the second rebellion made up for that. It supplied spirit and subject for no fewer than six compositions of varying degrees of interest and intensity. In fact, an entire book could be devoted to the lyrical fallout of the second Riel rebellion.

The twentieth century dawned with Canadian volunteers serving on foreign battlefields. *Voyageurs* rowed up the Nile, volunteers fought alongside Imperial troops in South Africa. If the first expedition was exotic, the second was an exercise in Imperial unity. The latter is the only war represented with an excruciatingly awful rhyme. "Kruger and the Boer War" was written by Ebenezer Bain, who published an entire book of such doggerel. Nor was he alone in this. Of all the battles in which Canadians have been engaged, the Boer War generated the most bad verse.

The effects of the Great War on modern man were profound, and have been the subject of innumerable studies, especially in literature. "In a not altogether rhetorical sense," noted writer Francis Hope, "all poetry written since 1918 is war poetry." The observation is profoundly true. Canada's participation in the First World War marked its coming of age. "There they stood on Vimy Ridge," orated Lord Byng. "Men from Quebec stood shoulder to shoulder with men from Ontario, men from the Maritimes with men from British Columbia, and there was forged a nation tempered by the fires of sacrifice and hammered on the anvil of high adventure." The troops crossed the Atlantic as colonials, and recrossed it as Canadians.

The same beginning marks literary modernism and modern Canadian nationalism. The 1914–18 war was the first in which Canadians wrote both poems and songs on the battlefield for other than patriotic and propagandistic purposes. When the combatants were poetically gifted, they left indelible records of their experiences, as surely as did the more widely appreciated War Artists, whose paintings, drawings, and sculptures are on permanent display in the National Gallery of Art in Ottawa.

A soldier at the second battle of Ypres composed one of the world's most memorized poems. The soldier was John McCrae and the poem was "In Flanders Fields," which at one time was learned by heart and recited on the steps of cenotaphs and pathways of cemeteries throughout the British Empire and Commonwealth of Nations. No ceremony on Remembrance Day since 1918 has been complete without its presence on the programme. And its presence there is ensured on every November eleventh into the foreseeable future.

Canadians were not official combatants in the Spanish Civil War; in fact, it was illegal for Canadians to enlist. Yet this was one war that engaged the attention of artists and intellectuals. A book could be compiled of the impassioned prose and poetry of Canadians and the civil war in Spain. Until that volume appears, the six poems printed here will have to give some notion of the quality of writing and thinking prompted by the struggle against fascism.

It was F. R. Scott who somewhat cynically noted that Canada won its independence mainly by fighting Germans. What is apparent, when one reads the songs, poems, and verses written during the Second World War, is that there is evidence here of a maturity and a sense of modernity found earlier nowhere else. No work was written that approached in popularity "In Flanders Fields" — although "High Flight" was known by heart by many — yet the new body of work stands by itself and may be read by anyone, whether a military buff or not, with considerable literary pleasure.

The Korean War, an unpopular one with the public, occasioned a handful of songs and poems. British and American bards celebrated the war in Korea hardly at all. But the Princess Pats fought well in that country, so three of their regimental songs are collected here. During the 1950s, 1960s, and 1970s, the Canadian people kept a watchful eye on the rest of the world, every so often casting a baleful glance in a southward direction. Canada was a bystander in the arenas of the world, and this is represented in the section devoted to Peacekeeping and Protest. The editors could find no poems directly inspired by Canada's United Nations peacekeeping operations, but they did find a great number of protest songs and poems, only a few of which are represented here. Perhaps it tells us something about the Canadian people, or about Canadian intellectuals, that there are more poems to protest the policies of the United States than the policies of the Soviet Union.

There is a symmetry in beginning the book with Indian Battles and ending it with Future Battles. No one knows what the future may bring, but one sure bet is that it will bring more battles. Not too many Canadian poets or songwriters have tried to face the future, but after much thought the present editors decided to conclude the book with a single poem, Earle Birney's chillingly titled prophecy "World War III." It is not a recent poem, for it was written in the immediate postwar years, in 1947. Things have not changed much, or for the better, in the decades since. Let us hope things will change more, and for the better, in the decades and centuries to come.

It is worthwhile to compare the lyrical utterances of the two world wars, for the comparison sheds light on the changes that have overtaken modern society. As well, since the poems and songs in these two sections comprise about two-thirds of this anthology's bulk, the comparison is generally revealing about modern Canadian war writing.

The president of the Royal Society of Canada in 1918 was William Douw Lighthall, lawyer, poet, mayor of Westmount, and wellknown anthologist of Canadian poetry. In his presidential address, he struck a poetic and patriotic note by using the occasion to read a selection of Great War poems written by Canadians. He also made some general points about the war and the opportunity it offered Canadians for dedication and self-sacrifice. The war afforded literary opportunities, perhaps the greatest in the history of the country. "This is our Homeric Age," he told his audience. "There never will be a greater fight. These never will be a vaster battlefield." He went on to say, "The Great War is vastly more stirring as an era than Confederation was. We are passing through the Valley of the Shadow of Death, and many of our sons have crossed the dark river itself and disappeared into the night." He noted, "Momentous views and profound feelings have already begun to find some utterance here as well as in other allied lands. By examining the body of scattered verse from Canadian pens, we may hope to construct a dim picture of our coming poetic generation." Then he added, "Never mind the form." He briefly examined the work of some poets, like John McCrae, who are represented in the present anthology, and a number of writers who patriotically versified the war, people like Canon Scott—Frederick George Scott, senior chaplain of the First Canadian Division, wounded at Cambrai, author of war verse, father of F. R. Scott. He even quoted Scott's inscription for the Soldiers' Monument at Quebec:

> Not by the power of Commerce, Art or Pen
>   Shall our great Empire stand, nor has it stood,
> But by the noble deeds of noble men,
>   Heroic lives and heroes' outpoured blood.

He ended by coming to terms with a new style of poetic utterance — "similar outbursts of utmost sincerity . . . with the ring of valour and the interest of truth." He quoted "The Taking of the Ridge" by Sapper J. T. Peck, which includes the following stanzas:

> For months we had stood a grilling fire
> From Fritz's guns across the mire,
> Our graveyards grew mid the bursting shell,
> The living breathed and tasted hell.
>
> Mud — the cursed Flanders mud: —
> Up to our necks and red with blood
> Barred the way to that coveted ridge
> Where the heaping corpses made a bridge.

Lighthall could sense in these lines the shaping of a new sensibility, one more matter-of-fact and modern.

No president of the Royal Society of Canada meeting in 1939–45 devoted an address to the poetic response to the call to arms. Conditions had profoundly changed. The public for poetry of the Robert W. Service and Pauline Johnson variety — narrative and ballad — was no longer a mass public, or at least it was no longer served by the mass media. Poetry in the twenties and thirties had been privatized. Earle Birney, who was an officer with the Canadian Army, surveyed some of the muse's productions in "To Arms with Canadian Poetry," a survey article published in the *Canadian Forum*, January 1940. There is not much sense in resurrecting the stanzas that Birney culls from *Saturday Night*, *Maclean's*, and other popular magazines of the day, in order to find them wanting in originality, for they are feeble efforts indeed. By and large the good poets were not publishing in the leading magazines; their work came out in little magazines and in book form, and long after the event, for a readership vastly inferior in size to the one enjoyed by the bards of the Great War. Birney dismissed all the verse he encountered, suggesting that the reader should wage a private war on "the seditious peace-rhymers." He concluded in an image apt for the times: "A Poetry Control Board is the order of the day." Lighthall had a vision of Homeric and limitless expanses, Birney a sense of quality control.

There is a marked difference in perspective between the serious poetry of the two world wars. Most of the poems written about the Great War are descriptions of scenes or actions. The most famous poem associated with that war, "In Flanders Fields," is essentially a description of what McCrae saw in the Belgian fields near Ypres. In the first stanza, the living see poppies, crosses, sky, larks, guns. In the second stanza, the dead experience dawn and sunset. In the third and last stanza, in a departure from the descriptive mode, the dead command the living to "take up the quarrel," moving from description into homily. The reader responds to all three stanzas, finding in the third the reason for the first and second. The poem is a description of a scene and the action is the compact to not "break faith." What remains is the image of the poppy, the symbol of the sleep of death and the need for remembrance.

The poets of the First World War described what they saw and what they believed, but not particularly what they sensed or felt. The poets of the Second World War were generally an introspective group. They did not encounter, when they took an inventory of their sensations and feelings and thoughts, a compact between the living and the dead. Consequently, no poem from the 1939–45 war may be directly compared with "In Flanders Fields." It is interesting to note that the only poem from the Second World War to compare with McCrae's poem is "High Flight." Adopted as an official poem by the Royal Canadian Air Force, it is only peripherally about the war. In fact, had not its author, John Gillespie Magee, Jr., died some months after writing it, it is doubtful the poem would even be associated with combat. It captures the excitement of sensation. It re-creates the feelings and sensations of flight — not fight — and it does so in muscular verbs: slipped, danced, climbed, joined, done, dreamed, wheeled, soared, swung. The physical ecstasy of the sensation of flight culminates in a vision, not of peace or brotherhood, king or country, but of the divine — "touched the face of God." The reference to the deity, which seems somewhat out of place, may be the culmination of the quest for complete sensation, for ecstasy.

Both "In Flanders Fields" and "High Flight" are romantic poems in the sense that they play on the emotions. Yet the one great casualty of the Great War was romanticism. It occurred later in Canadian literature than elsewhere, but in its wake went the mystique of war, patriotism, idealism. That is not to say the poets and singers in uniform in the so-called Hitler war were not patriotic or idealistic. Many were, but in this war there were atheists in the foxholes. This war was a job that had to be done, "the war to end war."

Poets were the reporters of the First World War, describing in stanzas the significance of sites of battle like Cambrai and Marne. In the Second World War, there was no need for versified adventure and rhymed patriotism — except perhaps in the inducement of war-bond drives — for Canada had a regiment of war correspondents, and radio kept listeners and readers informed.

Songs and poems are sometimes forged in the heat of battle, but most of the most moving ones were written long after the events they describe. The poets of the Second World War were not reporters; instead, they were witnesses. As witnesses, they reflected on their experiences, and the act of reflection takes time. Soldier-poets, like George Whalley and Douglas LePan, published their collections some years after the events described had transpired. In the case of Raymond Souster, the poems took up to four decades to emerge. The finest novel about a Canadian in the Great War appeared in 1977, almost sixty years after the fighting. The novel is Timothy Findley's *The Wars*. Not only was the author not a participant in that war, he was not even born until a dozen years after it ended.

Other points could be made, but perhaps it would be wise to end with a comparison instead of a contrast. Some things may change but others remain much the same. The songs that inspire men remain relatively alike. The most famous concert group to emerge from the Great War was the Dumbells, a troop of soldiers who toured the front lines and then the home front, and kept performing well into the 1930s. The troop, led by Colonel Merton Plunkett, had a lighthearted air and captured the hearts of service personnel and civilians. Witness this verse from the group's signature tune, "The Dumbell Rag," composed by Ivor E. Ayre:

> Oh that Dumbell Rag,
> That "Dummy" Dumbell Rag!
> Sing it high or sing it low,
> Just sing it together
> And let 'er go, Hi!

There is not all that much difference between the Dumbells and "The Happy Gang," the most popular radio programme on the Canadian airwaves in the 1930s, 1940s, and 1950s. Led by Bert Pearl, members of the Happy Gang contributed mightily to the war effort, singing patriotic and military songs, acting as friends and surrogate family members to its many radio listeners. It was broadcast five days a week, and hardly a programme was heard during the war years that did not feature its rendition of "There'll Always Be an England." The lyrics of this patriotic air are hardly known to the Baby Boomers, but no one born earlier will ever forget them. The song was published by Gordon V. Thompson in Toronto in 1939. The lyrics would not be amiss in the Great War. The refrain runs:

> Red, white and blue,
> What does it mean to you?
> Surely you're proud,
> Shout it aloud,
> Britons awake,
> The Empire too.

The poetry of the First World War was pictorial and patriotic. The poetry of the Second World War was physiological and psychological. And the poetry of all wars is pregnant with prophecy.

There are prophetic strains in all poetry, but they are especially prevalent in war poetry. Poets of the First World War expressed their belief in the continuity of high ideals — glory, valour — and poets of the Second World War stressed the resumption of reasonableness—"orderly decontrol." But specific predictions are seldom considered the province of prophecy.

There is a genuine act of prophecy, even of prediction, in one poem published in 1944. The author of the startlingly accurate prediction was A. M. Klein, who, too young to enlist in the First World War and too old to enlist in the Second, fulminated in Montreal against Adolf Hitler and the Nazi Party in *The Hitleriad* (1944) and also in the poem, "Psalm XXV," written in 1943. The prophecy, though couched in the ironic mode often characteristic of this great poet, concerned the manner of Hitler's death. The relevant lines are the following:

> They are upon us, the prophets, minor and major!
> Madame Yolanda rubs the foggy crystal.
> She peers, she ponders, the future does engage her;
> She sees the *Führer* purged by Nazi pistol.

Why soldiers should write more poetry than, say, doctors or lawyers, bricklayers or salesmen, is a moot point. Perhaps the reason they do was noted by Jon Stallworthy in *The Oxford Book of War Poetry* (1984). Next to love, war has provoked the widest range of emotions and, thus, some of the best poetry. This point was raised by Lieutenant Colonel C. W. Gilchrist in his foreword to *Rhyme and Reason*, a slim collection of verse published in Rome by the Canadian Public Relations Services in February 1945.

> Give a soldier a stub of lead pencil and a piece of paper and the first thing you know he's written a poem. Maybe all men are poets at heart and it just takes a war to awaken that hidden talent, for it is a fact that some really great poetry has been written by soldiers in this and other wars.
>
> Perhaps it is because there is plenty of time to think in the army. Those long vigils when dug in and waiting for something to happen, those black, bleak nights when sleep will not come, give plenty of opportunity to think — to look inside oneself.

It is then very often that, by the light of a guttering candle in some shell-blasted *casa* or in some nice cozy slit trench, poems are born. They do not come full-fledged, but haltingly—perhaps only a few words, a line or two, on the back of a tattered envelope or scribbled on a cigarette box.

When William Butler Yeats was asked to write a war poem, he declined the honour, noting: "I think it better that in times like these / A poet's mouth be silent, for in truth / We have no gift to set a statesman right. . . ." Yet had the Irish poet been conscripted to fight in one of England's wars, it is quite likely he would have concluded "On Being Asked for a War Poem" on a note other than the one he sounded: "He has had enough of meddling who can please / A young girl in the indolence of her youth, / Or an old man upon a winter's night."

It is doubtful that Rudyard Kipling, Yeats's contemporary—they were born the same year but died three years apart, Kipling in 1936, Yeats in 1939 — ever declined a request for a war poem. Indeed, upon request he contributed inscriptions for memorials throughout the British Empire, including those in Sudbury and Sault Ste. Marie and the Peace Chamber of the Houses of Parliament in Ottawa, the texts of which appear in this volume. He sat on the Imperial (later Commonwealth) War Graves Commission and chose the words that appear on the headstones of unknown Canadian soldiers who died in the First World War: A CANADIAN SOLDIER OF THE GREAT WAR / KNOWN UNTO GOD. He also selected, from the apocryphal Book of Ecclesiastes, the sentences that mark the centrepieces of many Commonwealth cemeteries for the fallen of the First and Second World Wars: THEIR NAME LIVETH FOR EVERMORE / LEUR NOM VIVRA À JAMAIS.

The literature of war, which encompasses the literature of the holocaust, may be the most extreme of any literature, and hence the most harrowing and compelling. It is also the most difficult to come to terms with. War, however much we detest it, remains a constant factor in human relations. It is as much a part of life as death is. To write about war is to write about the range of human emotions. It is to face the front line of human emotions and to find them conflicting. For every dedication there is a defeat, for every idealism there is cowardice, for excitement there is tedium, for glory there is gore and grime, for heroism there is hedonism, for sacrifice there is cynicism, for honour there is death. The poetry of war does not sing the destructive powers of man, but it does recognize the place of death in life, the need for sacrifice, the desirability and attainability of peace. No Canadian poet has yet written a poem as great as the Latin one that begins "Of arms and the man I sing," but they are on their way to doing so.

So this anthology of war poems and songs celebrates not so much the fighting spirit of man as it does the spirit of man in the service of his fellow man in the protection of the values of civilization.

It was frequently noted in the past that the refrain of "O Canada," the national anthem, included three repetitions of the line "We stand on guard for thee." Over the years the repetitions have been reduced to two. "God keep our land glorious and free!" replaces one of the "stand on guards." But Canadians still do guard duty — no doubt about it!

1

INDIAN BATTLES

Legion are the battles of the native people on this continent. The Indians of early Canada fought their own wars for centuries before the arrival of the newcomers from Europe. From the late fifteenth century on, the Indian did battle with and against the white man. Alliances were formed; the Algonquins and Hurons with the French, the Iroquois with the English. Thereupon the native warrior joined battles other than his own. The war dance gave way to the military march.

Europeans altered the balance of Indian power in 1609, when Samuel de Champlain, seeking to reward his Algonquin allies, joined one of their raiding parties in an assault against the Mohawks of the Iroquois Confederacy. The Iroquois of the confederacy subsequently sought support from the Dutch and English. For almost three centuries there were battles between native and newcomer and among native groups. They came to a halt, symbolically at least, in the last of the Métis uprisings in the West in 1885.

The Indians of the past were doughty warriors, and no account of Indian battles would be complete without praise for their qualities of courage and endurance, and their abilities as guerrillas. Warfare was no stranger to the Indian (as it was to the Eskimo, who sang no martial songs), and the word "war" may modify any number of nouns — "cry," "bonnet," "dance," "song" — with specific meaning.

The Iroquois were specially fierce fighters and their war songs showed it. Early ethnologists like Henry Rowe Schoolcraft placed the "Iroquois War Song" at the pinnacle of Iroquois and Indian eloquence. Schoolcraft was Indian agent at Sault Ste. Marie,

Michigan, in 1836 and the hospitable host of Anna Brownell Jameson. He arranged for Mrs. Jameson's induction into a Chippewa tribe and supplied her with translations of Iroquois lyrics. She reproduced a traditional "Iroquois War Song" in her classic travel book, *Winter Studies and Summer Rambles in Canada* (1838).

Two Indian raids are recalled in narrative verses included here. Archibald Lampman was inspired to write "At the Long Sault" by the expedition of Adam Dollard des Ormeaux against the Iroquois. Fighting commenced at an abandoned fort on the Ottawa River on May 1, 1660, and it lasted ten days. Adam Dollard (called Daulac in the poem), with sixteen companions and forty Huron and four Algonquin allies, held the fort against the assault of five hundred Iroquois, who finally took it and slew the defenders. Dollard's deed may or may not have saved the fledgling community of Ville Marie, today's Montreal, but it did inspire poets and nationalists, just as it inspired Lampman.

William Henry Drummond, the "habitant poet," found inspiration in the pluck and heroism of Madeleine de Verchères. In the absence of her parents, this fourteen-year-old girl defended the family seigneury on the St. Lawrence River against an Iroquois attack launched on October 22, 1692. With two younger brothers, two soldiers, and one family retainer, she held the fort eight days before relief finally arrived and the Iroquois withdrew. Like Dollard, young Madeleine became a symbol of sacrifice and resistance.

A surprising conclusion to this section on Indian Battles is supplied by "Watkwenies." This stark sonnet about an Indian warrior in her old age was written by Duncan Campbell Scott, the distinguished poet who retired from the civil service in Ottawa as deputy superintendent in the Department of Indian Affairs in 1932. It is more dramatic than strictly sympathetic, perhaps, but it does attempt to reveal the psychology of an old woman with a valiant past.

IROQUOIS WAR SONG

TRADITIONAL

I sing, I sing, under the centre of the sky,
    Under the centre of the sky,
Under the centre of the sky, I sing, I sing,
    Under the centre of the sky!

Every day I look at you, you morning star,
    You morning star;
Every day I look at you, you morning star,
    You morning star.

The birds of the brave take a flight round the sky,
    A flight round the sky;
The birds of the brave take a flight, take a flight,
    A flight round the sky.

They cross the enemies' line, the birds!
    They cross the enemies' line;
The birds, the birds, the ravenous birds,
    They cross the enemies' line.

The spirits on high repeat my name,
    Repeat my name;
The spirits on high, the spirits on high,
    Repeat my name.

Full happy am I to be slain and to lie,
    On the enemies' side of the line to lie;
Fully happy am I, full happy am I,
    On the enemies' side of the line to lie!

AT THE LONG SAULT: MAY, 1660

ARCHIBALD LAMPMAN

Under the day-long sun there is life and mirth
    In the working earth,
And the wonderful moon shines bright
    Through the soft spring night,
The innocent flowers in the limitless woods are springing
    Far and away
    With the sound and the perfume of May,
And ever up from the south the happy birds are winging,
    The waters glitter and leap and play
    While the grey hawk soars.

But far in an open glade of the forest set
    Where the rapid plunges and roars,
Is a ruined fort with a name that men forget, —
    A shelterless pen
    With its broken palisade,
    Behind it, musket in hand,
    Beyond message or aid
    In this savage heart of the wild,
    Mere youngsters, grown in a moment to men,
    Grim and alert and arrayed,
    The comrades of Daulac stand.
    Ever before them, night and day,
    The rush and skulk and cry
    Of foes, not men but devils, panting for prey;
    Behind them the sleepless dream
Of the little frail-walled town, far away by the plunging
    stream,
    Of maiden and matron and child,
With ruin and murder impending, and none but they
To beat back the gathering horror
Deal death while they may,
    and then die.

Day and night they have watched while the little plain
Grew dark with the rush of the foe, but their host
Broke ever and melted away, with no boast
But to number their slain;
And now as the days renew
Hunger and thirst and care
Were they never so stout, so true,
Press at their hearts; but none
Falters or shrinks or utters a coward word,
Though each setting sun
Brings from the pitiless wild new hands to the Iroquois
    horde,
And only to them despair.

Silent, white-faced, again and again
Charged and hemmed round by furious hands,
Each for a moment faces them all and stands
In his little desperate ring; like a tired bull moose
Whom scores of sleepless wolves, a ravening pack,
Have chased all night, all day
Through the snow-laden woods, like famine let loose;
And he turns at last in his track
Against a wall of rock and stands at bay;
Round him with terrible sinews and teeth of steel
They charge and recharge; but with many a furious
    plunge and wheel,
Hither and thither over the trampled snow,
He tosses them bleeding and torn;
Till, driven, and ever to and fro
Harried, wounded and weary grown,
His mighty strength gives way
And all together they fasten upon him and drag him down.

So Daulac turned him anew
With a ringing cry to his men
In the little raging forest glen,
And his terrible sword in the twilight whistled and slew.

And all his comrades stood
With their backs to the pales, and fought
Till their strength was done;
The thews that were only mortal flagged and broke
Each struck his last wild stroke,
And they fell one by one,
And the world that had seemed so good
Passed like a dream and was naught.

And then the great night came
With the triumph-songs of the foe and the flame
Of the camp-fires.
Out of the dark the soft wind woke,
The song of the rapid rose away
And came to the spot where the comrades lay,
Beyond help or care,
With none but the red men round them
To gnash their teeth and stare.

All night by the foot of the mountain
    The little town lieth at rest,
The sentries are peacefully pacing;
    And neither from East nor from West

Is there rumour of death or of danger;
    None dreameth tonight in his bed
That ruin was near and the heroes
    That met it and stemmed it are dead.

But afar in the ring of the forest,
    Where the air is so tender with May
And the waters are wild in the moonlight,
    They lie in their silence of clay.

The numberless stars out of heaven
    Look down with a pitiful glance;
And the lilies asleep in the forest
    Are closed like the lilies of France.

MADELEINE VERCHÈRES

WILLIAM HENRY DRUMMOND

I've told you many a tale, my child, of the old heroic days
Of Indian wars and massacre, of villages ablaze
With savage torch, from Ville Marie to the Mission of
    Trois-Rivières
But never have I told you yet, of Madeleine Verchères.

Summer had come with its blossoms, and gaily the robin sang
And deep in the forest arches the axe of the woodman rang.
Again in the waving meadows, the sun-browned farmers met
And out on the green St. Lawrence, the fisherman spread his
    net.

And so through the pleasant season, till the days of October
    came
When children wrought with their parents, and even the old and
    lame
With tottering frames and footsteps, their feeble labours lent
At the gathering of the harvest le bon Dieu himself had sent.

For news there was none of battle, from the forts on the
    Richelieu
To the gates of the ancient city, where the flag of King Louis flew
All peaceful the skies hung over the seigneurie of Verchères,
Like the calm that so often cometh, ere the hurricane rends the
    air.

And never a thought of danger had the Seigneur sailing away,
To join the soldiers of Carignan, where down at Quebec they lay,
But smiled on his little daughter, the maiden Madeleine,
And a necklet of jewels promised her, when home he should
    come again.

And ever the days passed swiftly, and careless the workmen grew
For the months they seemed a hundred, since the last war-bugle
    blew.
Ah! little they dreamt on their pillows, the farmers of Verchères,
That the wolves of the southern forest had scented the harvest
    fair.

Like ravens they quickly gather, like tigers they watch their prey
Poor people! with hearts so happy, they sang as they toiled away.
Till the murderous eyeballs glistened, and the tomahawk leaped
    out
And the banks of the green St. Lawrence echoed the savage
    shout.

"Oh mother of Christ have pity," shrieked the women in
    despair.
"This is no time for praying," cried the young Madeleine
    Verchères,

"Aux armes! aux armes! les Iroquois! quick to your arms and
    guns.
Fight for your God and country and the lives of the innocent
    ones."

And she sped like a deer to the mountain, when beagles press
    close behind
And the feet that would follow after, must be swift as the prairie
    wind.
Alas! for the men and women, and little ones that day
For the road it was long and weary, and the fort it was far away.

But the fawn had outstripped the hunters, and the palisades drew
    near,
And soon from the inner gateway the war-bugle rang out clear;
Gallant and clear it sounded, with never a note of despair,
'Twas a soldier of France's challenge, from the young Madeleine
    Verchères.

"And this is my little garrison, my brothers Louis and Paul?
With soldiers two — and a cripple? may the Virgin pray for us all.
But we've powder and guns in plenty, and we'll fight to the latest
        breath
And if need be for God and country, die a brave soldier's death.

"Load all the carabines quickly, and whenever you sight the foe
Fire from the upper turret, and the loopholes down below.
Keep up the fire, brave soldiers, though the fight may be fierce
        and long
And they'll think out little garrison is more than a hundred
        strong."

So spake the maiden Madeleine, and she roused the Norman
        blood
That seemed for a moment sleeping, and sent it like a flood
Through every heart around her, and they fought the red Iroquois
As fought in the old time battles, the soldiers of Carignan.

And they say the black clouds gathered, and a tempest swept the
        sky
And the roar of the thunder mingled with the forest tiger's cry
But still the garrison fought on, while the lightning's jagged spear
Tore a hole in the night's dark curtain, and showed them a
        foeman near.

And the sun rose up in the morning, and the colour of blood was
        he
Gazing down from the heavens on the little company.
"Behold! my friends!" cried the maiden, " 'tis a warning lest we
        forget
Though the night saw us do our duty, our work is not finished
        yet."

And six days followed each other, and feeble her limbs
        became
Yet the maid never sought her pillow, and the flash of the
        carabines' flame

Illumined the powder-smoked faces, aye, even when hope
    seemed gone
And she only smiled on her comrades, and told them to fight,
    fight on.

And she blew a blast on the bugle, and lo! from the forest black
Merrily, merrily ringing, an answer came pealing back.
Oh! pleasant and sweet it sounded, borne on the morning air,
For it heralded fifty soldiers, with gallant De la Monnière.

And when he beheld the maiden, the soldier of Carignan,
And looked on the little garrison that fought the red Iroquois
And held their own in the battle, for six long weary days,
He stood for a moment speechless, and marvelled at woman's
    ways.

Then he beckoned the men behind him and steadily they
    advance
And with carabines uplifted, the veterans of France
Saluted the brave young Captain so timidly standing there
And they fired a volley in honour of Madeleine Verchères.

And this, my dear, is the story of the maiden Madeleine.
God grant that we in Canada may never see again
Such cruel wars and massacres, in waking or in dream
As our fathers and mothers saw, my child, in the days of the old
    regime.

WATKWENIES

DUNCAN CAMPBELL SCOTT

Vengeance was once her nation's lore and law:
When the tired sentry stooped above the rill,
Her long knife flashed, and hissed, and drank its fill;
Dimly below her dripping wrist she saw
One wild hand, pale as death and weak as straw,
Clutch at the ripple in the pool; while shrill
Sprang through the dreaming hamlet on the hill,
The war-cry of the triumphant Iroquois.

Now clothed with many an ancient flap and fold,
And wrinkled like an apple kept till May,
She weighs the interest-money in her palm,
And, when the Agent calls her valiant name,
Hears, like the war-whoops her perished day,
The lads playing snow-snake in the stinging cold.

2

THE ENGLISH AND THE FRENCH

The French were the traditional rivals of the English on the European continent. So it is not surprising that they became foes on the continent of North America. The need to maintain the "balance of power" in the Old World was matched in the New World by the need to control trade routes, if not the fur trade itself.

There was a century and a half of conflict. It was characterized by clashes and campaigns, sorties and seiges, attacks and battles, thin red lines and guerrilla warfare. The battle lines were drawn across the eastern half of the continent. There was hostility in 1626–30 and again in 1666–67; there was open battle — King William's War in 1689–97, Queen Anne's War of 1702–13, King George's War of 1744–48, and the Seven Years' War of 1756–63. Hostilities of an armed sort came to an end with the fall of New France and subsequent rise of British North America.

Events that occurred prior to the Seven Years' War, the most significant period of warfare, are represented by the poem, "The Captured Flag." After Sir William Phips took Acadia, he made an unsuccessful assault on Quebec. On October 15, 1690, Phips's envoy delivered the ultimatum to Count Frontenac to surrender Quebec. Frontenac replied, "I have no reply to make to your general other than from the mouths of my cannon and muskets." The poem, "The Captured Flag," written by Arthur Weir, an Anglo-Canadian from Montreal, is unusual in that it tells of the assault from the French point of view.

The Seven Years' War, which lasted for seven years in Europe, extended over nine years in North America. Britain declared war on France in 1756, but the conflict had already begun two years earlier in the Ohio Valley. Hostilities ceased with France's succession of New France to Britain by the Treaty of Paris in 1763. There were significant French victories at Fort William Henry in 1757 and at Fort Carillon (also called Ticonderoga, New York) in 1758. The most significant British victories were at Louisbourg in 1758 and on the Plains of Abraham outside the walled city of Quebec on September 13, 1759.

The Seven Years' War is represented by a number of songs and poems. The first song is *"Amis chantons la gloire,"* by an unknown singer, which celebrates the victory of the French under Montcalm at Oswego, the English fort on the south bank of Lake Ontario, in the summer of 1756. In the unrhymed translation of Yves Zoltvany, it reads: "Friends sing the glory / Of our brave Frenchmen / Celebrate their victory / Celebrate their exploit / What will the prince think / When Machault [minister of marine] will tell him / Sire among your provinces / Long live Canada // Vaudreuil [governor of New France] by his prudence / Prevents accidents / Bigot [intendant] by foresight / Provides the ramparts / The soldier, the militia / Obedient to the general / For the good of the service / Fly at the first signal // Of New England / One of the strong bulwarks / Razed to the ground / Its standards pulled down / All its artillery / Its supplies, its vessels / And its infantry / Respect our banners // The waves of Lake Ontario / Are astonished / To see so many people / Surrender at this moment / Cease being surprised / Know that our warriors / On the waters of the Thames / Are conquering laurels."

The Battle of the Plains of Abraham was one of those fateful engagements that changed the face of history. By upsetting the balance of power in North America, it altered that in the Western world. The victory of Brigadier General James Wolfe and his nine thousand British troops over the fourteen thousand French soldiers commanded by the Marquis de Montcalm remains the turning point in the history of early Canada. The battle took place at 4:30 A.M., September 13, 1759. It was over in twenty minutes. Both generals died of wounds—Wolfe on the battlefield, Montcalm the following day.

There is a tradition that the night before the final battle, while sailing up the St. Lawrence to his rendezvous, Wolfe recited in a low voice to his silent men the one stanza of Gray's "Elegy Written in a Country Churchyard" that speaks of death. The stanza runs:

> The boast of heraldry, the pomp of pow'r,
> And all that beauty, all that wealth e'er gave,
> Awaits alike th'inevitable hour,
> The paths of glory lead but to the grave.

Wolfe paused, then added, "Gentlemen, I would rather have written those lines than take Quebec tomorrow." This must count as one of the most historic poetry recitals of all time. (It is based on the reminiscence of John Robison, a young midshipman, who later taught at the University of Edinburgh. Some historians, such as F. W. Whitton, dismiss it as a "legend": "For this preposterous perversion there is not a particle, a scintilla, an iota of evidence.")

The battle is represented not by Thomas Gray's "Elegy" but by the folk song "General Wolfe" collected by Edith Fowke in Ontario in 1957. Al Purdy's "Dead March for Sergeant MacLeod" adds a contemporary note to this famous event in world history.

THE CAPTURED FLAG

ARTHUR WEIR

Loudly roared the English cannon, loudly thundered back our
    own,
Pouring down a hail of iron from their battlements of stone,
Giving Frontenac's proud message to the clustered British ships:
"I will answer your commander only by my cannons' lips."
Through the sulphurous smoke below us, on the Admiral's ship
    of war,
Faintly gleamed the British ensign, as through cloud-wrack
    gleams a star;
And above our noble fortress, on Cape Diamond's rugged crest, —
Like a crown upon a monarch, like an eagle in its nest, —
Streamed our silken flag, emblazoned with the royal *fleur-de-lys*,
Flinging down a proud defiance to the rulers of the sea.
As we saw it waving proudly, and beheld the crest it bore,
Fiercely throbbed our hearts within us, and with bitter words we
    swore,
While the azure sky was reeling at the thunder of our guns,
We would strike that standard never, while Old France had
    gallant sons.

Long and fiercely raged the struggle, oft our foes had sought to
    land,
But with shot and steel we met them, met and drove them from
    the strand;
Though they owned them not defeated, and the stately Union
    Jack,
Streaming from the slender topmast, seemed to wave them
    proudly back.
Louder rose the din of combat, thicker rolled the battle smoke,
Through whose murky folds the crimson tongues of thundering
    cannon broke;
And the ensign sank and floated in the smoke-clouds on the
    breeze,

As a wounded fluttering sea-bird floats upon the stormy seas.
While we looked upon it sinking, rising, through the sea of
     smoke,
Lo! it shook, and bending downwards, as a tree beneath a stroke,
Hung one moment o'er the river, then precipitously fell,
Like proud Lucifer descending from high heaven into hell.
As we saw it flutter downwards, till it reached the eager wave,
Not Cape Diamond's loudest echo could have matched the cheer
     we gave;
Yet the English, still undaunted, sent an answering echo back;
Though their flag had fallen conquered, still their fury did not
     slack,
And with louder voice their cannon to our cannonade replied,
As their tattered ensign drifted slowly shoreward with the tide.

There was one who saw it floating, and within his heart of fire,
Beating in a Frenchman's bosom, rose at once a fierce desire,
That the riven flag thus resting on the broad St. Lawrence tide
Should, for years to come, betoken how France humbled
     England's pride.
As the stag leaps down the mountain, with the baying hounds in
     chase,
So the hero, swift descending, sought Cape Diamond's rugged
     base,
And within the water, whitened by the bullets' deadly hail,
Springing, swam towards the ensign with a stroke that could not
     fail.
From the shore and from the fortress we looked on with bated
     breath,
For around him closer, closer, fell the messengers of death;
And as nearer, ever nearer, to the floating flag he drew,
Thicker round his head undaunted still the English bullets flew.
He has reached and seized the trophy! Ah! what cheering rent
     the skies,
Mingled with deep English curses, as he shoreward brought his
     prize!
Slowly, slowly, almost sinking, still he struggled to the land,

And we hurried down to meet him as he reached the welcome
    strand;
Proudly up the rock we bore him, with the flag that he had won,
And that night the English vessels left us with the setting sun.

AMIS CHANTONS LA GLOIRE
UNKNOWN

Amis chantons la gloire
De nos braves Français
Célébrons leur victoire
Célébrons leur exploit
Qu'en pensera le prince
Quand Machault lui dira
Sire entre vos provinces
Vive le Canada

Vaudreuil par sa prudence
Y prévient le hasard
Bigot par prévoyance
Y fournit les remparts
Le soldat, la milice
Soumis au général
Pour le bien du service
Vole au premier signal

De la Neuve Angleterre
Un des forts boulevards
Mis à niveau de terre
Tirer ses étendards
Toute l'artillerie
Ses vivres, ses vaisseaux
Et son infanterie
Respectent nos drapeaux

D'Ontario les ondes
Sont dans l'étonnement,
De voir que tant de monde
Se rendent en ce moment
Cessez votre surprise
Sachez que nos guerriers
Sur l'eau de la Tamise
Remportent des lauriers.

GENERAL WOLFE

TRADITIONAL

Oh, General Wolfe to his men did say,
"Come, come, my boys, come follow me
To yon blue mountain that stands so high,
You lads of honour, you lads of honour,
You lads of honour, come follow me.

"Don't you see the French on yon mountains high
While we poor fellows in the valleys lie?
You'll see them falling from our guns
Like motes a-flying, like motes a-flying,
A-falling from our great British guns."

The very first volley the French fired at us
They wounded our general on his left breast.
Yonder he sat for he could not stand.
"Fight on so bravely, fight on so bravely,
For while there's life I shall give command.

"When to old England you do return,
You tell my friends that I'm dead and gone,
And tell my tender old mother dear
To weep not for me, to weep not for me,
For I died a death that I wished to share.

" 'Twas sixteen years when I first begun
All for the honour of George the King.
You commanders all, do as I've done before,
Be a soldier's friend, my boys, be a soldier's friend, my boys,
And then you'll fight for ever more."

DEAD MARCH FOR SERGEANT MACLEOD

AL PURDY

(Seventy years old, wounded and returning to England from Quebec with the corpse of General Wolfe in 1759)

The sea outside is the river
St. Lawrence and the boxed corpse
once General Wolfe and the wide mouth
of the gulf is a womb of death and the lap
lap lap of water is memory memory
of drums and guns and smoking guns
outside Quebec the dead are shovelled
and buried each with a lithograph
in his head and heart and brain
of the last thought the last glass
of wine the last woman the last
small lead ball growing and growing
and becoming a mountain at last
becoming smaller being nothing
And what about you General sir
in a coffin in the hold of the Royal
William draped in a flag does Gray's
Elegy still seem very important now
to you in your pine box at any rate
what about God whose existence is not
beyond doubt puttering around
in a workshop jammed with hypotheses
you with your weak body and chinless

face fixed fast with its last commands
like stones shyed back from nowhere?
And you Sergeant Macleod
are there wars ready
and waiting for you to arrive adrenalin
stored in your head musket balls
firing indiscriminate pop pop pop?
Old killer on the battlefields of Europe
old amputator of arms and legs and daylight
staring at Wolfe's corpse admiringly
what do you say sergeant
any advice for new recruits now
and how do you speak to Generals even
if they're dead and don't hear a word
only the waves outside going lap lap lap
idiot music idiot questions idiot God?
 — rockabye Skye baby rockabye home
inside the wooden walls of the womb of things
where we have been and where we are going
when we are not —

3

THE AMERICAN INVASION

The story goes that the first two acts of the Continental Congress, convened in Philadelphia in 1774, concerned Canada. The first act of Congress was to issue an invitation to Quebec to become "the Fourteenth Colony." The second act, when the first was ignored, was to order the invasion of Quebec.

Among the leaders of the volunteer American expeditionary forces that entered Canada were Ethan Allen, Benedict Arnold, and Richard Montgomery. Sir Guy Carleton defended Montreal, which fell to the Americans on November 13, 1775, and then he withdrew to Quebec, which he held with three hundred British regulars and eighteen hundred men. The Americans blockaded the walled town, and Montgomery was mortally wounded as he attempted an assault on the ramparts on December 31, 1775. The Americans maintained a blockade until the arrival of the first supply ship from Britain in the spring. They withdrew on May 6, 1776, and by the end of the following month Canada was clear of American occupation.

The American invasion of Canada is recalled in a song and a poem. "Marching Down to Old Quebec" is a children's song that was collected by Edith Fowke in 1957. It is said to celebrate the withdrawal of Americans from Montreal, but in its original American version (the third and fourth lines run: "The American boys have won the day, / And the British are retreating") was sung by their troops as they made their way from Montreal to Quebec. "Spirit of 1775–1975" by Raymond Souster puts the supreme sacrifice of Richard Montgomery into a contemporary context.

MARCHING DOWN TO OLD QUEBEC

TRADITIONAL

Oh, we're marching down to old Quebec
And the fifes and the drums are a-beating,
For the British boys have gained the day,
And the Yankees are retreating,
So we'll turn back and we'll come again
To the place where we first started,
And we'll open the ring and we'll take a couple in,
Since they proved that they are true-hearted.

SPIRIT OF 1775-1975

RAYMOND SOUSTER

General Richard Montgomery, American commander:
"I'll have my Christmas dinner in Quebec
or die in the attempt."

So died in the attempt,
along with many of his men, the strips of paper
reading "Liberty or Death" they carried in their caps
buried with their corpses in the snows of Lower Town.

1775, year of the first invasion
of Canada by the Yankees. Losers at first,
they never quite gave up trying: even General Brock
couldn't stem the tide forever.

Now by 1975
they've completely conquered us,
not with arms
but with dollars,
not with love
but by sharp Yankee trading.

General Richard Montgomery, American commander,
never got his Christmas dinner
in Quebec City. Instead, a few years later,
Benjamin Franklin got the 49th Parallel
and the Ohio Valley, which he reckoned rightly
was worth a defeat or two, many Christmas dinners. . . .

4

THE WAR OF 1812

The War of 1812 was a conflict between Great Britain and the United States that occurred on sea and land, with the principal engagements in Upper and Lower Canada, Louisiana, and Washington, District of Columbia. The Americans declared war on the British on June 19, 1812, ostensibly to protest the searching of American ships on the high seas, but really to check British rivalry in the fur trade and to seize British North America. The next thirty months saw no end of sorties, campaigns, invasions, raids, and seiges. The heroic deaths of Sir Isaac Brock and the Shawnee chief Tecumseh in Upper Canada, and the courage shown by Laura Secord (whose deed was not offically recognized until 1860), settled into Anglo-Canadian annals of history and patriotism. The signing of the Treaty of Ghent on December 25, 1914, brought an end to the war and restored the status quo by providing for the establishment of a boundary commission to determine the international border between the two countries.

"Come All You Bold Canadians" recalls General Brock's initial victory. General Hull surrendered Detroit on August 15, 1812. The Battle of Queenston Heights, which overlooks the Niagara River, was the most dramatic campaign of the war. American invaders were repulsed on October 13, 1812, but General Brock was mortally wounded. The battle is recalled in a song of the day and a poem (by Francis Sparshott) of our day.

"Tecumseh's Death" is an account of the last battle fought by the Shawnee chief Tecumseh, who died at the Battle of Moraviantown (near Thamesville, Ontario) on October 6, 1813.

The account in verse was written by Major John Richardson, novelist and veteran of the campaign. There are some forgotten references in the work. The "Christian" is Colonel Johnston, the leader of the Kentucky Riflemen, who drew a pistol from his belt and killed Tecumseh just as the latter was about to tomahawk him.

"The Chesapeake and the Shannon" is a ballad about a naval engagement that took place outside Boston Harbour on June 1, 1813. The captain of the HMS Shannon was Philip Bowes Vere Broke, and the captain of the USS Chesapeake was James Lawrence. Lawrence taunted Broke, and the engagement was quickly concluded, with the Shannon overpowering the Chesapeake. Lawrence was mortally wounded. His dying words have gone down in American history: "Blow her up! Sink her! Don't give up the ship!" But the Chesapeake was not sunk; it was towed by the Shannon into Halifax Harbour.

For the rededication of Brock's Monument at Queenston Heights, Charles Sangster wrote his poem, "Brock." It is one of the few formal dirges or elegies inspired by a Canadian occasion. The editors of the present collection had hoped to include a ballad about the exploit of Laura Secord in trekking through the woods by night to warn the British of the impending American attack, June 21–22, 1813. Charles Mair's "A Ballad for Brave Women" presented itself, but the work is so weak it hardly seemed appropriate to the occasion. Instead, the editors included a very contemporary sideways glance at Laura Secord by Raymond Souster.

For the lyrics of the most famous song inspired by an incident during the War of 1812, the reader will have to turn elsewhere. Unquestionably the best-known song is the U.S. National Anthem, "The Star-Spangled Banner," the lyrics of which were written by an American lawyer, Francis Scott Key, who watched as the British bombarded Fort McHenry in Boston Harbour. The naval bombardment took place September 13–14, 1814, and Key woke the next morning heartened to see the American flag still flying over the fort. He wrote four eight-line verses and titled it "Defence of Fort McHenry." It was later set to an old tune, "To Anacreon in Heaven," and called "The Star-Spangled Banner." Although widely sung on ceremonial occasions, and adopted as the anthem of the U.S. Army and Navy, it was not recognized as the American

National Anthem by the U.S. Congress until 1931. The first
verse goes like this:

O! say can you see by the dawn's early light,
What so proudly we hail'd at the twilight's last gleaming,
Whose broad stripes and bright stars, through the perilous fight,
O'er the ramparts we watched were so gallantly streaming?
And the rocket's red glare, the bombs bursting in air,
Gave proof through the night that our flag was still there;
O! say does that star-spangled banner yet wave,
O'er the land of the free, and the home of the brave?

COME ALL YOU BOLD CANADIANS

TRADITIONAL

Come all you bold Canadians, I'd have you lend an ear
Concerning a fine ditty that would make your courage cheer,
Concerning an engagement — that we had at Sandwich town,
The courage of those Yankee boys so lately we pulled down.

There was a bold commander, brave General Brock by name,
Took shipping at Niagara and down to York he came,
He says, "My gallant heroes, if you'll come along with me,
We'll fight those proud Yankees in the west of Canaday!"

'Twas thus that we replied: "Along with you we'll go.
Our knapsacks we will shoulder without any more ado.
Our knapsacks we will shoulder and forward we will steer;
We'll fight those proud Yankees without either dread or fear."

We travelled all that night and a part of the next day,
With a determination to show them British play.
We travelled all that night and a part of the next day,
With a determination to conquer or to die.

Our commander sent a flag to them and unto them did say:
"Deliver up your garrison or we'll fire on you this day!"
But they would not surrender, and chose to stand their ground,
We opened up our great guns and gave them fire a round.

Their commander sent a flag to us, a quarter he did call.
"Oh, hold your guns, brave British boys, for fear you slay us all.
Our town you have at your command, our garrison likewise."
They brought their guns and ground them right down before our
    eyes.

And now we are all home again, each man is safe and sound.
May the memory of this conquest all through the Province sound!
Success unto our volunteers who did their rights maintain,
And to our bold commander, brave General Brock by name!

THE BATTLE OF QUEENSTON HEIGHTS

TRADITIONAL

Upon the Heights of Queenston one dark October day,
Invading foes were marshalled in battle's dread array.
Brave Brock looked up the rugged steep and planned a bold
    attack;
"No foreign flag shall float," said he, "above the Union Jack."

His loyal-hearted soldiers were ready every one,
Their foes were thrice their number, but duty must be done.
They started up the fire-swept hill with loud resounding cheers,
While Brock's inspiring voice rang out: "Push on, York
    Volunteers!"

But soon a fatal bullet pierced through his manly breast,
And loving friends to help him around the hero pressed;
"Push on," he said, "Do not mind me!" — and ere the set of sun
Canadians held the rugged steep, the victory was won.

Each true Canadian soldier laments the death of Brock;
His country told its sorrow in monumental rock;
And if a foe should e'er invade our land in future years,
His dying words will guide us still: "Push on, brave Volunteers!"

THE BALLAD OF QUEENSTON HEIGHTS

FRANCIS SPARSHOTT

The Yankees stood on Queenston Heights
in coats of modest grey
and Brock has brought his fencibles
to make them go away

Who is that sweating officer
waving a useless sword?
That's General Sir Isaac Brock
who wants to be a Lord

God bless the British soldier
who wears a coat of red
it makes a splendid target
and so they shot him dead

They laughed to see the fencibles
run down the hill in fear
but Roger Sheaffe has scaled the Heights
and caught them in the rear

Who is this cool young officer
who shoots us through the heart?
That's Major General Roger Sheaffe
who wants to be a Bart

Now all you bold Canadian girls
remember Queenston Heights
it's thanks to such as Brock and Sheaffe
that you sleep safe at nights

Cool Sheaffe was made a Baronet
and back to England sent
but Brock still stands on Queenston Heights
upon his monument

TECUMSEH'S DEATH

MAJOR JOHN RICHARDSON

Amid that scene, like some dark towering fiend,
   With death-black eyes and hands all spotted o'er,
The fierce Tecumseh on his tall lance leaned,
   Fired with much spoil and drunk with human gore;
And now his blasting glance ferocious gleamed —
   The chief who leads the eagles to his shore —
When, with one scream that devils might appal,
Deep in his breast he lodged the whizzing ball.

Like the quick bolt that follows on the flash
   Which rends the mountain oak in fearful twain,
So springs the warrior with infernal dash
   Upon the Christian writhing in his pain;
High gleamed his hatchet, ready now to crash
   Along the fibres of his swimming brain,
When from the adverse arm a bullet flew
With force resistless, and with aim too true.

The baffled Chieftain tottered, sunk, and fell,
   Rage in his heart, and vengeance in his glance;
His features ghastly pale — his breast was hell;
   One bound he made to seize his fallen lance,
But quick the death-shades o'er his vision swell,
   His arm dropped nerveless, straining to advance;
One look of hatred, and the last, he gave,
Then sunk and slumbered with the fallen brave.

Forth from the copse a hundred foemen spring,
   And pounce like vultures on the bleeding clay;
Like famished bloodhounds to the corse they cling,
   And bear the fallen hero's spoils away;
The very covering from his nerves they wring,
   And gash his form, and glut them o'er their prey, —
Wild hell-fiends all, and revelling at his death,
With bursting shrieks and pestilential breath.

THE *Chesapeake* AND THE *Shannon*

TRADITIONAL

The *Chesapeake* so bold out of Boston as we're told
Came to take the British frigate neat and handy O,
And the people in the port all came out to see the sport
While their bands all played up Yankee Doodle Dandy O!

Before this action had begun, the Yankees made much fun,
Said, "We'll tow her up to Boston neat and handy O!
And after that we'll dine, treat our sweethearts all with wine,
And we'll dance a jig of Yankee Doodle Dandy O."

Our British frigate's name that for the purpose came
To cool the Yankees' courage neat and handy O
Was the *Shannon* — Captain Broke, all his crew had hearts of oak
And in fighting were allowed to be the dandy O.

The fight had scarce begun when they flinched from their guns;
They thought that they had worked us neat and handy O;
But Broke he waved his sword, saying, "Come my boys, we'll
        board,
And we'll stop them playing Yankee Doodle Dandy O."

When Britons heard this word they all quickly sprang on board
And seized the Yankees' ensign neat and handy O.
Notwithstanding all their brags, the British raised their flags
On the Yankee's mizzen-peak to the dandy O!

Here's to Broke and all his crew, who with courage stout and true
Fought against the Yankee frigate neat and handy O.
O may they ever prove both in fighting and in love
That the British tars will always be the dandy O!

BROCK

CHARLES SANGSTER

October 13, 1859

One voice, one people, one in heart
 And soul, and feeling, and desire!
 Re-light the smouldering martial fire,
 Sound the mute trumpet, strike the lyre,
 The hero deed can not expire,
  The dead still play their part.

Raise high the monumental stone!
 A nation's fealty is theirs,
 And we are the rejoicing heirs,
 The honoured sons of sires whose cares
 We take upon us unawares,
  As freely as our own.

We boast not of the victory,
 But render homage, deep and just,
 To his — to their — immortal dust,
 Who proved so worthy of their trust
 No lofty pile nor sculptured bust
  Can herald their degree.

No tongue need blazon forth their fame —
 The cheers that stir the sacred hill
 Are but mere promptings of the will
 That conquered then, that conquers still;
 And generations yet shall thrill
  At Brock's remembered name.

Some souls are the Hesperides
 Heaven sends to guard the golden age,
 Illuming the historic page
 With records of their pilgrimage;
 True Martyr, Hero, Poet, Sage:
  And he was one of these.

Each in his lofty sphere sublime
    Sits crowned above the common throng.
    Wrestling with some Pythonic wrong,
    In prayer, in thunder, thought, or song;
    Briaereus-limbed, they sweep along,
    The Typhons of the time.

LAURA SECORD

RAYMOND SOUSTER

Lady, long part of our history,
would you perhaps have been so eager
that time to drive those silly cows
before you through the forest mile on mile,
risking who-knows-what indignities
at the hands of the invaders,

had you known you would end up
the name on the box for a brand
of over-sweet chocolates?

5

THE MASSACRE OF SEVEN OAKS

The main cause of the Massacre of Seven Oaks was the commercial rivalry between the two fur-trade giants of the West, the Hudson's Bay Company and the North West Company. The massacre took place on June 19, 1816; sixty Métis under Cuthbert Grant, supported by the North West Company, killed some twenty settlers, including Robert Semple, governor of Assiniboia, at the Red River settlement, which was on land granted by the Hudson's Bay to Lord Selkirk some four years earlier. The settlers withdrew under threat of further action. The site of the massacre is marked today in downtown Winnipeg.

Present at the massacre was the Métis singer Pierre Falcon (1793–1876), Grant's brother-in-law and North West employee who, the following day, composed "The Battle of Seven Oaks." The French version first appeared in print in 1871, and James Reaney's English translation was originally published in 1960. Reaney explained: "I have attempted to make only an English equivalent of Falcon's ballad and so translate the really important thing — its high spirits."

THE BATTLE OF SEVEN OAKS

PIERRE FALCON

Would you like to hear me sing
Of a true and recent thing?
It was June nineteen, the band of Brois-Brûlés
    Arrived that day,
      Oh the brave warriors they!

We took three foreigners prisoners when
We came to the place called Frog, Frog Plain.
They were men who'd come from Orkney,
    Who'd come, you see,
      To rob our country.

Well we were just about to unhorse
When we heard two of us give, give voice.
Two of our men cried, "Hey! Look back, look back!
    The Anglo-Sack
      Coming for to attack."

Right away smartly we veered about
Galloping at them with a shout!
You know we did trap all, all those Grenadiers!
    They could not move
      Those horseless cavaliers.

Now we like honourable men did act,
Sent an ambassador — yes, in fact!
"Monsieur Governor! Would you like to stay?
    A moment spare —
      There's something we'd like to say."

Governor, Governor, full of fire.
"Soldiers!" he cries, "Fire! Fire."
So they fire the first and their muskets roar!
    They almost kill
      Our ambassador!

Governor thought himself a king.
He wished an iron rod to swing.
Like a lofty lord he tries to act.
 Bad luck, old chap!
 A bit too hard you whacked!

When we went galloping, galloping by
Governor thought that he would try
For to chase and frighten us Bois-Brûlés.
 Catastrophe!
 Dead on the ground he lay.

Dead on the ground lots of Grenadiers too.
Plenty of Grenadiers, a whole slew.
We've almost stamped out his whole army.
 Of so many
 Five or four left there be.

You should have seen those Englishmen —
Bois-Brûlés chasing them, chasing them.
From bluff to bluff they stumbled that day
 While the Bois-Brûlés
 Shouted "Hurray!"

Tell, oh tell me who made up this song?
Why it's our own poet, Pierre Falcon.
Yes, she was written this song of praise
 For the victory
 We won this day.
Yes, she was written, this song of praise —
 Come sing the glory
 Of the Bois-Brûlés.

6

THE REBELLION OF 1837

The Rebellion of 1837 was born of the frustration felt by *patriotes* in Lower Canada and militant reformers in Upper Canada when their grievances against autocratic government practices were met with indifference. The leaders of the insurrections were Louis-Joseph Papineau in Lower Canada and William Lyon Mackenzie in Upper Canada.

The insurrection in Lower Canada, today's Quebec, lasted sporadically from October 24, 1837, to November 10, 1838. British regulars and the Canadian militia were required at Saint-Charles, Saint-Denis, and Saint-Eustache. Following the fighting there were twelve executions for treason and fifty-eight *patriotes* were exiled to penal servitude in New South Wales.

The insurrection in Upper Canada, today's Ontario, was quelled by the Canadian militia — the British regulars were engaged in Lower Canada. The fighting lasted from December 4, 1837, to December 3, 1838. In the aftermath there were twenty executions — including that of Lount and Matthews on April 12, 1838 — and one hundred and nineteen militant reformers were sent to Tasmania.

It was not until 1849 that a full amnesty for all participants was proclaimed.

The rebellion in Lower Canada is represented by two songs and one narrative in verse. Sir George Etienne Cartier, a *patriote* of '37, a Father of Confederation in '67, wrote the words and music of "*Avant tout je suis Canadien*," which was the marching song of the Sons of Liberty (whom Cartier dubbed "Sons of Victory"). A literal prose translation of the lyrics was supplied by John Boyd:

"Often they boast of the customs and laws of Great Britain: France and Spain, on account of their wines, have a right to our praises; to admire the skies of Italy and to laud Europe is all very well, but for me I prefer my own country. Before all I am a Canadian." (Perhaps *Canadien* is preferable to Canadian.)

"De Papineau Gun," the verse narrative, was written by William Henry Drummond in the patois of the *habitant*, his specialty. It recounts an incident that occurred involving Papineau and a fellow rebel leader, Wolfred Nelson. "Un Canadien Errant," the moving song, was composed and sung by Antoine Gérin-Lajoie in 1842, when he was eighteen years old. It remains popular to this day. Indeed, the historian Benjamin Sulte wrote: "Sing that poetry in any place you wish on the face of the continent, and if a French Canadian happens to stand within hearing distance (which is likely to be the case), he will come to you."

The lyrics of "Un Canadien Errant" have defied translation. John Boyd prepared an English version which runs: "Weeping sorely as he journeyed / Over many a foreign strand, / A Canadian exile wandered, / Banished from his native land. // Sad and pensive, sitting lonely / By a rushing river's shore, / To the flowing waters spake he / Words that fondest memories bore: // "If you see my own dear country — / Most unhappy is its lot — / Say to all my friends, O river, / That they never are forgot. // "Oh! those days so full of gladness, / Now forever are they o'er, / And alas! my own dear country, / I shall never see it more. // "No, dear Canada, O my homeland! / But upon my dying day, / Fondly shall my last look wander / To thee, beloved, far away."

There are two lyrics and one poetic lament to represent the rebellion in Upper Canada. The lyrics are complementary in that they present the opposing sides of the "late unpleasantness." Both appeared in 1838 and offer the reader—and singer—new verses to "God Save the King." The Patriot side is represented by "Lord! Free Us All!" and the Loyalist side by "National Anthem." The poetic lament is a haunting two-part poem by Raymond Souster.

AVANT TOUT JE SUIS CANADIEN

SIR GEORGE ETIENNE CARTIER

Souvent de la Grande Bretagne,
On vante et les moeurs et les lois;
Par leurs vins, la France et l'Espagne
A nos éloges ont des droits.
Admirez le ciel d'Italie
Louez l'Europe c'est fort bien;
Mois, je préfère ma patrie:
Avant tout je suis Canadien.

"DE PAPINEAU GUN" — AN INCIDENT OF THE CANADIAN REBELLION OF 1837

WILLIAM HENRY DRUMMOND

Bon jou, M'sieu' — you want to know
    'Bout dat ole gun — w'at good she's for?
W'y! Jean Batesse Bruneau — mon pere,
    Fight wit' dat gun on Pap'neau War!

Long tam since den you say — C'est vrai,
    An' me too young for 'member well,
But how de patriot fight an' die,
    I offen hear de ole folk tell.

De English don't ack square dat tam,
    Don't geev de habitants no show,
So 'long come Wolfred Nelson
    Wit' Louis Joseph Papineau.

An' swear de peep mus' have deir right.
   Wolfred he's write Victoriaw,
But she's no good, so den de war
   Commence among de habitants.

Mon pere he leev to Grande Brulé.
   So smarter man you never see,
Was alway on de grande hooraw!
   Plaintee w'at you call "Esprit!"

An' w'en dey form wan compagnie
   All dress wit' tuque an' ceinture sash
Ma fader tak' hees gun wit' heem
   An' marche away to Saint Eustache,

W're many patriots was camp
   Wit' brave Chenier, deir Capitaine,
W'en 'long come English Generale,
   An' more two t'ousan' sojer man.

De patriot dey go on church
   An' feex her up deir possibill;
Dey fight deir bes', but soon fin' out
   "Canon de bois" no good for kill.

An' den de church she come on fire,
   An' burn almos' down to de groun',
So w'at you t'ink our man can do
   Wit' all dem English armee roun'?

'Poleon, hees sojer never fight
   More brave as dem poor habitants,
Chenier, he try for broke de rank
   Chenier come dead immediatement.

He fall near w're de cross is stan'
   Upon de ole church cimitiere,
Wit' Jean Poulin an' Laframboise
   An' plaintee more young feller dere.

De gun dey rattle lak' tonnere
    Jus' bang, bang, bang! dat's way she go,
An' wan by wan de brave man's fall
    An' red blood's cover all de snow

Ma fader shoot so long he can
    An' den he's load hees gun some more,
Jomp on de ice behin' de church
    An' pass heem on de 'noder shore.

Wall! he reach home fore very long
    An' keep perdu for many days,
Till ev'ry t'ing she come tranquille,
    An' sojer man all gone away.

An' affer dat we get our right,
    De Canayens don't fight no more,
Ma fader's never shoot dat gun,
    But place her up above de door.

An' Papineau, an' Nelson too
    Dey're gone long tam, but we are free,
Le Bon Dieu have 'em 'way up dere.
    Salut, Wolfred! Salut, Louis!

UN CANADIEN ERRANT

ANTOINE GÉRIN-LAJOIE

Un Canadien errant,
Banni de ses foyers,
Parcourait en pleurant
Des pays étrangers.

Un jour, triste et pensif,
Assis au bord des flots,
Au courant fugitif
Il adressa ces mots:

"Si tu vois mon pays,
Mon pays malheureux,
Va, dis à mes amis
Que je me souviens d'eux.

"O jours si pleins d'appas,
Vous êtes disparus,
Et ma patrie, hélas!
Je ne la verrai plus.

"Non, mais en expirant,
O mon cher Canada,
Mon regard languissant
Vers toi se portera."

LORD! FREE US ALL!

ANONYMOUS

Lord! o'er our own loved land
Spread thy protecting hand!
    Help! ere we fall!
Free us from Monarchy —
Free us from Hierarchy,
Sabres and *Squirearchy* —
    Lord, free us all!

O, men of England! rise!
Arm for the precious prize,
    Your birthright, all!
With firm heart, with iron-hand
As *One* let *Millions* stand,
A true and steadfast band —
    Triumph, or fall!

Lord! o'er our own loved land,
Spread thy protecting hand!
    Help! ere we fall!
Free us from tyrant-knaves —
Let us no more as slaves
Find our inglorious graves, —
    Lord; free us all!

NATIONAL ANTHEM

ANONYMOUS

Lord, on our side be seen,
Prosper our rightful Queen,
    Bless our young Queen!
Her loyal people bless,
And give their swords success,
Shield us from all distress;
    God save the Queen!

Put down th' invading band
Threat'ning our happy land,
    Mocking our Queen.
Set every fear at rest,
Animate each breast;
On thee our cause we rest:
    God save the Queen!

SEPARATE INSCRIPTIONS FOR THE GRAVES OF LOUNT AND MATTHEWS

RAYMOND SOUSTER

(Necropolis Cemetery, Toronto)

I

I, Samuel Lount, coming from Pennsylvania
to find work, live a free man,
found work but no freedom.
So, fashioning a pike in the forge,
I marched down Yonge Street,
proud of it as a banner.
Though the hand was struck down
I hope that metal still glows.

II

I, Peter Matthews, having fought the Yankees
with the Brock volunteers, sniffed out worse tyranny
thickening here, an insufferable cesspool.
Reluctantly, turning my plough into a sword,
I hacked at the leg-irons chaining us all,
but found only justice
dangling from a British noose.

7

THE FENIAN RAIDS

The Fenian Raids of 1866–70 were mounted by the American branch of the Irish Revolutionary Brotherhood, which sought to strike at England by attacking Canada, and thus bring about the independence of Ireland. The name Fenian recalls the body of warriors who roamed the Irish countryside in the distant past.

The Canadian militia encountered some difficulty repulsing the Fenian raiding parties, which ranged in strength from eighteen hundred to a few hundred. There were raids on Campobello Island, New Brunswick; Fort Erie and Prescott, Ontario; Pigeon Hill and Eccles Hill in Quebec's Eastern Townships; and Pembina, Manitoba. The American authorities soon put a stop to the raids because they were a breach of neutrality. Their effect encouraged the British colonies to confederate in 1867.

The Fenian Raids inspired a plethora of verse and song. The verse included here, "The Fenian Blood-Hounds," written by one W. Case, comes from a broadside printed and distributed in Upper Canada in 1866.

THE FENIAN BLOOD-HOUNDS

W. CASE

Dedicated to Sweeny & O'Mahony.

Come on, ye poor deluded dupes,
    And listen to this song;
Come on — and one good flogging get —
    It will not take us long.

Because our Volunteers turn'd out
    Like Lions! from the den;
Not like the coward, Fenian hearts,
    But with the hearts of men.

Come on — come on — we anxious wait
    To meet you on our shore;
Where you will soon be satisfied
    That "Fenians" are no more!

It is our blood these wretches seek,
    Their looks are mark'd with murder —
They march — and march — towards the lines,
    But darsn't come — no furder!

No Fenian dupes shall own our soil —
    Our flag still waves on high;
And never shall that flag fall down
    Until we all shall die!

Why loiter on the other side?
    Or do you want more aid?
The weather likely is too cold
    As yet, to make a "raid!"

The Fenians here in Canada
    Await the time to join —
To get a perfect drilling — like
    The "Battle of the Boyne!"

And only wait like lurking wolves
    That prowl around by night,
To murder — burn up children — wives —
    Whose men are gone to fight.

They have collected mammoth funds,
    And dupes — blood-thirsty scum —
With cannon, rifles, pikes, and swords —
    Why don't the cowards come?

But should the battle day arrive,
    Then onward to the field;
Let guardian angels bear the flag,
    And God will be our shield.

8

THE MOUNTED POLICE

The Royal Canadian Mounted Police are a recognized symbol of Canada around the world. The federal government established the force as a civil police for service in the Northwest on May 23, 1873. The original name was the North West Mounted Police. The prefix "Royal" was granted in 1904, and the name was changed to the present one (with the initials RCMP) in 1920. In Quebec, the force is called *Gendarmerie royale du Canada*. The force's motto is *Maintiens le droit*, or, "Uphold the Right." (The unofficial motto is "They Always Get Their Man.") Since 1920, the force has acted as the federal police force, the provincial police force in eight of the ten provinces, and the municipal police force in many communities throughout the country.

The Mounted Police are recognized in this collection with "The Riders of the Plains," the earliest, the longest, and the best-known tribute to the force. It appeared in the September 23, 1878, issue of the *Saskatchewan Herald*, published in Battleford, and it was signed "*W.S., N.W.M.P.*" Research has failed to establish the identity of the versifier. The verse is reprinted from *Wake the Prairie Echoes* (1973), a collection of poems about the force collected by the Saskatchewan History and Folklore Society.

The editors of the present collection, readers will realize, stood their ground and manfully resisted the impulse to reprint selected lyrics from *Rose-Marie*, the 1924 Broadway operetta about the force. Its principal attraction is the lilting melodies composed by Rudolf Friml, not the inane words written by Otto Harbach and Oscar Hammerstein II. Yet they can never dissever their image of the force from the scene in the 1936 Hollywood movie *Rose Marie*, in which Nelson Eddy croons to Jeanette MacDonald, "Oh, Rose Marie, I love you! / I'm always dreaming of you. . . ."

Canadians are made of sterner stuff than Sergeant Malone, played by Nelson Eddy, and to this day members of the force call a soft assignment "a Rose Marie posting." When Canadians sing the repeated refrain of the national anthem, the line "We stand on guard for thee" should conjure up the scarlet and the stetson and the Mounted Policeman, for he (and these days she) stands on guard in the literal and figurative senses of the word in times of war and peace.

THE RIDERS OF THE PLAINS

UNKNOWN

Oh! let the prairies echo with
    The ever-welcome sound —
Ring out the boots and saddles,
    Its stinging notes resound.
Our horses toss their bridled heads.
    And chafe against the reins —
Ring out — ring out the marching call
    For the Riders of the Plains.

O'er many a league of prairie wide
    Our pathless way must be;
And round it roams the fiercest tribes
    Of Blackfoot and of Cree.
But danger from their savage hands
    Our dauntless hearts disdain —
The hearts that bear the helmet up —
    The Riders of the Plains!

The thunderstorm sweeps o'er our way,
    But onward still we go;
We scale the weary mountains' range,
    Descend the valleys low;
We face the broad Saskatchewan,
    Made fierce with heavy rains —
With all its might it cannot check
    The Riders of the Plains.

We track the sprouting cactus land,
    When lost to white man's ken,
We startle there the creatures wild
    And fight them in their den;
For where'er our leaders bid,
    The bugle sounds its strains,
In marching sections forward go
    The Riders of the Plains.

The Fire King stalks the broad prairie,
    And fearful 'tis to see
The rushing wall of flame and smoke
    Girdling round rapidly.
'Tis there we shout defiance
    And mock its fiery chains —
For safe the cleared circle guards
    The Riders of the Plains.

For us no cheerful hostelries
    Their welcome gates unfold —
No generous board, or downy bed,
    Await our troopers bold.
Beneath the starry canopy
    At eve, when daylight wanes,
There lie the hardy slumberers —
    The Riders of the Plains.

But that which tries the courage sore
    Of horseman and of steed,
Is want of blessed water —
    Blessed water is our need.
We'll face, like men, whate'er befalls,
    Of perils, hardships, pains —
Oh! God, deny not water to
    The Riders of the Plains!

We muster but three hundred
    In all this Great Lone Land,
Which stretches from Superior's waves
    To where the Rockies stand;
But not one heart doth balk,
    No coward voice complains,
That far too few in numbers are
    The Riders of the Plains.

In England's mighty Empire
    Each man must take his stand:

Some guard her honoured flag at sea,
  Some bear it well by land.
It's not our part to face her foes —
  Then what to us remains?
What duty does our country give
  To the Riders of the Plains?

Our mission is to plant the right
  Of British freedom here —
Restrain the lawless savages,
  And protect the pioneer.
And 'tis a proud and daring trust
  To hold these vast domains
With but three hundred mounted men —
  The Riders of the Plains.

W.S., N.W.M.P.

Cobourg, July 1878

9

THE RIEL REBELLIONS

The Riel Rebellions were two in number; twice the Métis people resorted to armed resistance to protect their land and their way of life. Their enemy was the federal government led by Sir John A. Macdonald, which was intent on incorporating the West into the newly formed Dominion of Canada. Louis Riel, the Métis leader, was a controversial and complex person who entertained a mystical view of his half-breed people and their relationship with the land and destiny.

Sir John A. Macdonald saw Riel as a troublemaker, then as a traitor, and the two rebellions—the Red River Rebellion of 1869–70 and the Northwest Rebellion of 1884–85—as acts of treason to be quickly suppressed. Riel attempted armed resistance first in Fort Garry, in modern-day Manitoba, and then in Batoche, in present-day Saskatchewan. Both attempts of the Métis to declare independence were suppressed by volunteers from Ontario.

General Garnet Wolseley led the expeditionary force against the Métis at Fort Garry. The rebellion collapsed on August 24, 1870, when Riel fled to Montana. The expeditionary force of 1885, led by General Frederick Middleton, faced sterner opposition in the guerrilla-style fighting of the Indians and the Métis under Riel's military commander, Gabriel Dumont. The turning point in the Northwest Rebellion was the Battle of Batoche, fought on May 9–12, 1885. Again Riel fled, but this time, after three days, he surrendered, mistakenly assuming that his innocence would be established by a court of law. Instead, he was found guilty of high treason and hanged at Regina on November 16, 1885.

The poems and songs inspired by the Northwest Rebellion are

more numerous and interesting than those inspired by the Red River Rebellion fifteen years earlier. "The Toronto Volunteers" is the marching song of the Queen's Own Rifles for this campaign. It was collected by Edith Fowke in Ontario some seventy years after the event. "The Man with the Gatling Gun" has no known author. The Gatling gun—an early, crank-operated machine gun—broke the back of the rebellion at Batoche, where it was used to fire up to five hundred rounds of ammunition a minute. The Métis were reduced to stuffing their muzzle-loaders with gravel and nails. The remaining poems, written by J. W. Bengough, Al Purdy, Raymond Souster, and Frederick George Scott, round out the representation given the Riel Rebellions.

THE TORONTO VOLUNTEERS

TRADITIONAL

In the year of Eighty-five, sure the tidings did arrive
To the city of Toronto it appeared,
From those snowy plains afar where those roving Indians are,
For assistance from our brave volunteers.

Oh those volunteers did go and face the storms and snow
With frost-bit toes and hard frozen ears,
And when the drums did beat, how those rebels did retreat!
It was fun for our brave volunteers.

THE MAN WITH THE GATLING GUN

UNKNOWN

Full many a line of expressions fine
    And of sentiments sweet and grand
Have been penned of "our boys" who, from home's dear joys,
    Set out for the North-West land.
We've been told how they've fought for the glory sought,
    We've heard of the deeds they've done;
But it's quite high time for some praise in rhyme
    For the man with the Gatling gun.

Music hath charms, even midst war's alarms,
    To soothe the savage breast;
None can hold a candle to that "music by Handel"
    That lulled Riel's "breeds" to rest,
And they sleep that sleep profound, so deep,
    From which shall awaken none;
And the lullabies that closed their eyes
    Were sung by the Gatling gun.

All honour's due — and they have it, too —
  To the Grens. and Q.O.R.
They knew no fear but, with British cheer,
  They charged and dispersed afar
The rebel crew; but 'twixt me and you
  When all is said and done,
A different scene there might have been
  But for Howard and his Gatling gun.

THE CHARGE AT BATOCHE

J. W. BENGOUGH

Who says that British blood grows tame,
  And that the olden fire is gone
That swept the fields of deathless fame
  When heroes led our soldiers on?
Let tyrant Czars, grown great on wrong,
  Believe that fable if they will,
While I rehearse in martial song
  A story of Canadian skill —
  And Canada is British still!

In Duty's name we lay before the pits
  All day, like targets for the rebel lead,
Wasting our bullets on the sullen hill,
  In whose grim side the enemy was hid.
In Duty's name we choked our anger down,
  And clenched our rifles in impatient grasp,
Blazing at random — waiting for the word —
  While comrades round us gave their dying gasp.

    Out rang the signal shrill,
      Each soldier's heart to thrill,
Along the line the inspiring signal — Charge!

All eager sprang the gallant Ninetieth then,
Up flashed the scarlet of each Royal Gren,
Forth thundered Boulton's scouts and French's men,
On dashed brave Howard's gatling in the van —
    'Twas Charge! Charge! Charge!

With rousing British cheers,
The loyal volunteers
    Swept grandly on!
Blenched at the whirlwind dread,
The shattered rebels fled —
    Batoche was won!
   Batoche was bravely won!

Won! but ah, dearly won those steeps,
   For on the field, in manhood's pride,
Lay heroes whom our country weeps —
   It was for Canada they died;
For Canada, fair Canada,
   Our gallant heroes fought and died.

Who says that British blood grows tame,
   Or that the olden fire is gone,
Must first forget Batoche's name,
   And how that day was fought and won!

THE BATTLEFIELD AT BATOCHE

AL PURDY

Over the earthworks among slim cottonwood trees
wind whistles a wind tune
I think it has nothing to do with living or dead men
or the price of groceries
it is only wind

And walking in the wooded dish-shaped hollow
that served to protect generals and staff
officers from sniper fire
I hear a different kind of murmur
— no more than that at least not definitely
the sort of thing you do hear
every now and then in a city never
questioning because it's so ordinary
but not so ordinary here
I ask my wife "Do you hear anything?"
She smiles "Your imagination again?"
"All right then don't you wish you had one?"
"If I did I'd burn your supper . . ."
the sort of thing she says to annoy me
the unanswerable kind of remark
that needs time to think about
I take my time watching the green curve
of the South Saskatchewan River below
a man riding an inch-long machine a mile distant
that makes dark waves cutting the yellow wheat
I wonder if Gunner Phillips heard the sound
on the day of May 12 in 1885
before the bullet knocked him down
the stairs he spent twenty years climbing?
Did Letendre with his muzzle-loader
clamped under one arm stuffing gun powder
down the barrel and jamming in a bullet
stop remembering great itchy beasts
pushing against log palisades at night
and running the buffalo at Grand Coteau
the Sioux screaming insults from a safe distance
at men from the White Horse Plain?
— all this in dream pantomime
with that sound and nothing else?
And old Ouellette age 90
his hearing almost gone anyway
wiping off river mist from his rifle
listening — ?

Under my feet grass makes small noises
a bright-eyed creature I can't identify
is curious about me
and chitters because it's August
In May the annoyed general eats his lunch
on the cliffs ordering "a reconnaissance in force"
his officers misinterpret as "attack in force"
Midlanders   Winnipeg Rifles   Grenadiers
move out from their own positions
and burst into the Metis rifle pits
with Captain Howard from Connecticut
a demonstrator for the Colt Firearms Company
of Hartford demonstrating
death at 500 rounds a minute
with the borrowed Gatling gun
But it wasn't the sound I hear now
not the dead shifting positions underground
to dodge bullets stopped in mid-earth
here a little way under the black soil
where wheat yellow as a girl's hair blossoms
the Metis nation was born and died
as the last buffalo stumbles to his knees
and felt cold briefly while his great wool
blanket was ripped from bloody shoulders
It is for Parenteau and Desjarlais
Ah-si-we-in of the Woods Crees
for Laframboise and old Ouellette
and dark girls left alone
that such words as mine are spoken
and perhaps also for Gunner Phillips
in his grave above the South Saskatchewan
but most for myself
And I say to my wife, "Do you hear nothing?"
"I hear the poem you're writing" she says
"I knew you were going to say that" I say
In evening listening
to the duplicate rain-sound on the roof
of our camped trailer it seems

that I was wrong about my motives
and the dark girls mourning at Batoche
the dead men in shallow rifle pits
these mean something
the rain speaks to them
the seasons pass
just outside their hearing
but what they died for has faded away
and become something quite different
past justice and injustice
beyond old Ouellette and his youngest grandson
with the larking dog chasing a rabbit
green grass growing
rain falling
on the road cars passing by
Like the child I am/was I say "Me too"
camped on the battlefield of Batoche
just slightly visible in August
me an extension of anything that ever happened
a shadow behind the future
the bullets aimed at me
by Gunner Phillips and old man Ouellette
eighty-five years ago
whispering across the fields of eternity

RIEL, 16 NOVEMBRE, 1885

RAYMOND SOUSTER

"Rome is fallen": Riel,
rousing the Métis for the last time

Walked at Batoche
among the rifle-pits
carrying a crucifix
and hoping for a miracle.

But never a gun,
"I do not like war."

Always beware the leader
who talks with God
and leaves you to do the dirty work.

IN MEMORIAM

FREDERICK GEORGE SCOTT

Those Killed in the North-West, 1885

Growing to full manhood now,
With the care-lines on our brow,
We, the youngest of the nations,
With no childish lamentations,
Weep, as only strong men weep,
For the noble hearts that sleep,
Pillowed where they fought and bled,
The loved and lost, our glorious dead!

Toil and sorrow come with age,
Manhood's rightful heritage;
Toil our arms more strong shall render,
Sorrow make our heart more tender,
In the heartlessness of time;
Honour lays a wreath sublime —
Deathless glory — where they bled,
Our loved and lost, our glorious dead!

Wild the prairie grasses wave
O'er each hero's new-made grave;
Time shall write such wrinkles o'er us,
But the future spreads before us
Glorious in that sunset land —
Nerving every heart and hand,
Comes a brightness none can shed,
But the dead, the glorious dead!

Lay them where they fought and fell;
Every heart shall ring their knell,
For the lessons they have taught us,
For the glory they have brought us.
Tho' our hearts are sad and bowed,
Nobleness still makes us proud —
Proud of light their names shall shed
In the roll-call of our dead!

Growing to full manhood now,
With the care-lines on our brow,
We, the youngest of the nations,
With no childish lamentations,
Weep, as only strong men weep,
For the noble hearts that sleep
Where the call of duty led,
Where the lonely prairies spread,
Where for us they fought and bled,
Our ever loved and glorious dead.

10

THE NILE EXPEDITION

The Nile Expedition of 1884, an unusual episode in the military history of the British Empire, marked the first time that a contingent of Canadians took part in an overseas war.

General Lord Wolseley, put in command of an expedition to ascend the Nile and bring relief to General C. G. ("Chinese") Gordon at Khartoum, recalled the skill and speed of the *voyageurs* who had assisted him in the Red River Rebellion of 1870. Their abilities might ensure the success of the rescue mission by covering the 860 miles of rapids and cataracts in record time.

A corps of 378 boatmen — French, English, Indian, Métis — enlisted for six months and went to the Sudan under Lieutenant Colonel Frederick Denison. The *voyageurs* sped up the Nile and approached the besieged city of Khartoum on January 28, 1885. They arrived too late, for two days earlier the Madhi had stormed the city and slain General Gordon. Some of the boatmen returned to Canada in March 1885; others re-enlisted for another six months and served for the remainder of the campaign.

THE CANADIANS ON THE NILE

WILLIAM WYE SMITH

O, the East is but the West, with the sun a little hotter;
And the pine becomes a palm, by the dark Egyptian water;
And the Nile's like many a stream we know, that fills its
    brimming cup, —
We'll think it is the Ottawa, as we track the batteaux up!
    Pull, pull, pull! as we track the batteaux up!
    It's easy shooting homeward, when we're at the top!

O, the cedar and the spruce, line each dark Canadian river;
But the thirsty date is here, where the sultry sunbeams quiver;
And the mocking mirage spreads its view, afar on either hand;
But strong we bend the sturdy oar, towards the Southern land!
    Pull, pull, pull! as we track the batteaux up!
    It's easy shooting homeward, when we're at the top!

O, we've tracked the Rapids up, and o'er many a portage
    crossing;
And it's often such we've seen, though so loud the waves are
    tossing!

11

THE BOER WAR

The South African War, which is the preferred name for the Boer War, was waged between Great Britain (with its colonies and dominions) and two Boer republics, the South African Republic (Transvaal) and the Orange Free State. Hostilities commenced on October 11, 1899, and concluded with the defeat of the Boer farmers. The Boer War was ended by a treaty signed on May 31, 1902.

The Boer War was a British imperial war, and Canadian opinion was divided on its response to the British call to arms. Indeed, French and some English Canadians wondered if Empire solidarity required a Canadian contingent of troops — the British strength was five hundred thousand men against the Boer's eighty-eight thousand. Ultimately the federal government sent volunteers to South Africa, but they served under overall British command and expense. A total of 7,300 Canadians fought with distinction at Paardeberg, Bloemfontein, Leliefontein, and Mafeking. (One of them was Lieutenant John McCrae of the Royal Canadian Artillery.) Casualties amongst the Canadian troops were light — eighty-eight died in action — but an additional one hundred and thirty-six succumbed to illness or accident.

This conflict is represented with a patriotic verse and a poetic meditation. The verse is by Ebenezer Bain, a belligerent, who wrote the lines "in the early part of the Boer War, 1900." The meditation is a contemporary one written by Don Coles, a native of Woodstock, Ontario.

KRUGER AND THE BOER WAR

EBENEZER BAIN

Paul Kruger, though not just a saint,
  Yet loves his Bible well;
His creed is pure, without a taint,
  He has no thought of Hell;
For he can read his title clear
  To mansions in the skies;
So smokes his pipe, and knows no fear,
  And British power defies.

For hath the Lord not mindful been
  Of Oom Paul Kruger's race,
And given the Afric tribes that teem
  As their inheritance?
So, with the Bible in one hand,
  And rifle in the other,
His faith is muscular and grand,
  Like Joshua, — a brother.

Religious frenzy, it is true,
  Is but insanity;
And Kruger madly threatens to
  "Stagger Humanity!"
Perhaps you may, conceited fool,
  But if you do, be sure
'Twill be the end of your misrule,
  And treachery of the Boer.

For now the British Lion is roused,
  And fierce and loud doth roar;
And with him, see his sturdy whelps
  To fight the crafty Boer.
They come from far Australian ranch,
  And from New Zealand strand,
From Canada, and India,
  To lend a helping hand.

Now woe to thee, thou sullen Boer,
   And all thy foreign knaves,
Whose hate and envy ill endure
   The power that frees the slaves.
Our Union Jack once more unfurl'd —
   What power can haul it down?
While freemen smile o'er all the world,
   And only tyrants frown.

The flag of Queen Victoria
   (We hail it with three cheers)
Shall wave o'er proud Pretoria,
   In spite of foes or fears;
While Kruger, with his men of war
   And hordes of foreign knaves,
Shall bite the dust, and bow before
   The Flag that rules the waves.

ON A BUST* OF AN ARMY CORPORAL KILLED ON HIS TWENTY-FIRST BIRTHDAY DRIVING A MUNITIONS WAGON IN THE BOER WAR

DON COLES

Ten feet up atop a slim stone column
His face, neatly bearded, forage cap
Tidily centred, stares out over the town's
Bowling green. His decent demeanour precludes
The phallic reference — Freud's coeval,
He is innocent of much that we have agreed
To know. This summer he has been here

*In Port Elgin, Ontario

Eighty years. Beneath him, now as in most
Summer evenings all this while, 80-year-olds
In straw fedoras and roomy trousers trundle
Their bowls up & down the trimmed and illuminated
Lawns. Their ages are as unchanging as his,
Their conversations are of the seasons,
Their fashions a matter of apparent obdurate
Conviction. For eighty years their random
Old-folks' wisdom, their windy laughter, their
Thrifty movements have entered his vision,
Risen to his hearing from these murmurous lawns.
Winters some die, turn, though elsewhere,
To stone as he did, alternates take over.
This summer a few of them might, finally, have been
His children. Late at night he sees them enter
The empty green, hears the suppressed click
Of bowls, the floated discreeter voices. And
Finds it odd, still, those distant, paused horsemen,
That roaring hurt, reins gone slack,
In Africa.

12

THE FIRST WORLD WAR

Britain's declaration of war on Germany, signed on August 4, 1914, brought Canada into what was called the Great War. A Canadian Expeditionary Force of thirty-three thousand volunteers was raised and within two months contingents began to leave for England. Four infantry divisions served in France. These were eventually grouped into the Canadian Corps, which, for the first time in 1917, was headed by a Canadian, Lieutenant General Sir Arthur Currie. It was discovered that the Canadians made excellent shock troops.

On cenotaphs across the country are engraved the names of little-known places that served as the sites of well-known battles. Among them are Amiens, Ancre Heights, Arras, Cambrai, Canal du Nord, Courcelette, Drocourt-Quànt, Festubert, Givenchy, Hill 70, Mons, Mont Houy, Passchendaele, Regina Trench, St. Eloi, The Somme, Valenciennes, Vimy, and Ypres, to list but French and Belgian place names. The name of Vimy was writ large, for here all four divisions of the Canadian Corps fought with special brilliance, taking the ridge on Easter Monday, April 9, 1917.

The Armistice was signed on November 11, 1918. Canada contributed to the Great War 619,636 officers and men from all services, of whom 59,544 lost their lives. Remembrance Day ceremonies, which mark the signing of the Armistice, commemorate the fallen of both the first and the second world wars.

The songs, poems, and verses that follow have a general thematic and chronological arrangement. They should give some idea of what it was like to be in uniform in the Great War.

Near the end of this section will be found the poem that is (with the possible exception of Kipling's "Recessional") the most famous of all war poems. "In Flanders Fields" was written in twenty minutes by Lieutenant John McCrae of the Canadian Army Medical Corps in the early morning of May 3, 1915, during the second battle of Ypres, Belgium. Its composition took place at an exposed medical dressing station near the Yser Canal during a check in the arrival of the wounded. The soldier-physician-poet was in deep sorrow. The previous day he had buried a young friend, Lieutenant Alexis Helmer, and the poem was written out of this personal sorrow. "In Flanders Fields" waited half a year to appear in print. It was published anonymously in *Punch* on December 8, 1915. McCrae died of double pneumonia on January 28, 1918, and lies in Wimereux Communal Cemetery, near Boulogne, France. Sir Arthur Currie, commander of the Canadian Corps, attended his funeral. "In Flanders Fields" was recited as part of the official Armistice Day programme on November 11, 1918, and has since become an integral part of all Remembrance Day ceremonies in Canada and in many other parts of the English-speaking world. The choice of the poppy as the memorial flower for the fallen was inspired by this poem. It has inspired, as well, numerous "replies" or "answers," including the one included here by Edna Jaques, which appears in school readers and was recited at the unveiling of the Tomb of the Unknown Soldier in Arlington National Cemetery, Washington, D.C.

WRONG TURN AT SARAJEVO

RAYMOND SOUSTER

"Stop, fool! You're going the wrong way,"
General Potiorek shouted at the driver
of the Archduke's car.

But for one Gavrilo Princip
waiting on the crowded pavement
in front of Schiller's store
it was the *right* way; his revolver
fired once, twice, three, four times,

the first shot through the car,
striking Sophie's corset and her right side,
another piercing
Franz Ferdinand's high coat collar,
severing the jugular vein
and coming to a stop in his spine.

"Soferl, don't die,
live for my children," the Archduke cried,
blood spurting from his lips.

That blood would not be checked,
would flow on through four endless years.

"WE ARE COMING, MOTHER BRITAIN"

WILFRED CAMPBELL

(Excerpt)

We are coming, Mother Britain,
   Full five hundred thousand strong,
We are coming, loyal, sturdy, heart and hand,
   We have sent two hundred thousand
And we're sending more along
   To rally round the loved old land.

WE ARE THE ROYAL HIGHLANDERS

ANONYMOUS

We are The Royal Highlanders, we come from Montreal,
We come from good old Westmount, and some from Cote St.
   Paul,
And when we get to Germany, we'll show them we're the best.
We're the boys to stop the bullets with the Molson's on our
   chest.

So let's away to Germany will be our battle cry,
So let's away to Germany, we'll drink before we die,
And when we get to Germany, we'll show them we're the best,
We're the boys to stop the bullets with the Molson's on our chest.

And when we get a new recruit, we'll take the beggar in,
We'll take him down to the Armoury and get him a uniform,
And when we get him a uniform, we'll show him he's the best.
He's the boy to stop the bullets with the Molson's on his chest.

THE EASTER PARADE, 1915

R. S. WEIR

The crowd goes up and down the street,
    In ones and twos and threes:
White-spatted girls, sleek-hatted men,
    Women in silken ease, —
    But I look not twice at these.

The khaki lads stroll down the street,
    In ones and twos and threes;
(And I see the rush from trench to trench
    Beyond the blood-red seas!)
    Ah! thrice I look at these.

AFTER THE SPEECHES
ABOUT THE EMPIRE

TED PLANTOS

April 17, 1915

I remember the Union-Jack-waving crowds
before our train pulled out, and the quiet later
that choked their gaiety — how they went black
and motionless white when the last photograph was taken

I volunteered with twenty-one others
August of '14 it was, and we were handsome then
in our red tunics, trousers as blue
as the ocean we ached to cross
and white helmets marching to the railway station

Sam Hughes couldn't have hoped for more
They were joining up right across Canada

In Vancouver we burned the Kaiser in effigy,
soaked him in kerosene and applauded the flames

The crowds cheered us in our new uniforms
when we marched ahead of automobiles,
horses and buggies and the local fire brigade
loaded down with flags

One of the officers told me
the war would last only three months,
and I'd likely not see any action

After the speeches about the Empire
soaked up our hearts and were over,
the band played "God Be With You Till We Meet Again"

And the crowded platform
went motionless quiet
when the train with us out the windows pulled away

Some Songs of the CEF

ANONYMOUS

These are some songs of the Canadian Expeditionary Force.
"The CEF was a marching army and most of its songs were sung
on the march," wrote one participant, "so much so that, in
England, the local people called them the 'Singing Canadians.' "

1. WE ARE SAM HUGHES' ARMY

(To the tune of "The Church's One Foundation")

We are Sam Hughes' Army,
No bloody good are we.
We cannot work, we cannot fight,
And why the hell should we?
And when we get to Berlin,
The Kaiser he will say,
"Hoch, hoch, Mein Gott,
What a bloody, rummy lot
Is Sam Hughes' Army!"

2. OH, WE ARE THE BOYS

Oh, we are the boys from the mountains and the prairie,
We are Canucks, you see.
We come from the East and we come from the West
To fight for the land of the free.
And now we're here with the rest of Britain's sons
And we don't give a damn for the Kaiser and his Huns.
We are the Canucks, you see.

3. THEY SAY WE'RE GOING OVER THE OCEAN

(To the tune of "My Bonnie Lies Over the Ocean")

They say we're going over the ocean,
They say we're going over the sea,
They say we're going over the ocean,
But it all sounds like B.S. to me.
B.S., B.S., it all sounds like B.S. to me.

4. KISS ME GOODNIGHT, SERGEANT MAJOR

Kiss me goodnight, Sergeant-Major,
Tuck me in my little wooden bed.
We all love you, Sergeant-Major,
When we hear you bawling, "Show a leg!"

Don't forget to wake me in the morning,
And bring around a nice hot cup of tea.
Kiss me goodnight, Sergeant-Major,
Sergeant-Major be a mother to me!

5. I WANT TO GO HOME

I want to go home. I want to go home.
The whizzbangs they rattle, the cannon they roar,
I don't want to go to the Front any more!
Take me over the sea, where the Allemand can't get at me —
Oh my, I don't want to die, I want to go home.

I want to go home. I want to go home.
I don't want to crouch in a trench any more,
When flying pigs hurtle and Jack Johnsons roar.
Take me over the sea, where snipers cannot snipe at me,
Oh my, I'm too young to die, I want to go home.

6. SING ME TO SLEEP

Sing me to sleep, where the bullets fall —
Let me forget the war and all.
Deep is my dugout, cold my feet,
Nothing but biscuits and bulley to eat.
Sing me to sleep where shells explode,
And shrapnel and "sausages" are la mode.

Over the sandbags you'll find —
Corpses before you and corpses behind.

Far, far from Ypres, I long to be,
Where German snipers can't snipe at me.
Think of me crouching where the lice creep,
Waiting for someone to sing me to sleep!

Sing me to sleep in the same old shed,
Where rats are running over my head.
Stretching out on my waterproof,
Dodging the rain that pours through the roof.
Sing me to sleep where the star-shells glow,
Full of French bear and café à l'eau,
Dreaming of home and the girl I love best —
Somebody's muddy trench boots on my chest!

Far, far from Ypres I want to be,
Where German snipers can't shoot at me.
Deep is my dugout, and wet are my feet.
Send me a whizbang, and put me to sleep.

7. WHEN THIS CRUEL WAR IS OVER

(To the tune of "Oh, What a Friend We Have in Jesus")

When this cruel war is over,
Oh, how happy I will be,
No more soldiering for me,
No more church parades on Sunday,
No more asking for a pass,
We will tell our Sergeant-Major
To stick the passes up his ass.
All the non-coms will be Navvies,
All the Officers as well;
When I get my civvy clothes on,
Tell them all to go to hell.

IT'S A LONG WAY TO TIPPERARY

It's a long way to Tipperary.
It's a long way to go.
It's a long way to Tipperary,
To the sweetest girl I know.
Goodbye, Piccadilly,
Farewell, Leicester Square,
It's a long, long way to Tipperary,
But my heart's right there.

This is the version of the famous marching song sung by the Princess Pats.
Words by Harry H. Williams, music by Jack Judge. The marching song was
written for a pub concert and first publicly performed on January 31, 1912,
more than two years before the outbreak of the Great War with which it
became identified.

MADEMOISELLE FROM ARMENTIÈRES

Mademoiselle from Armentières, parlez-vous?
Mademoiselle from Armentières, parlez-vous?
Mademoiselle from Armentières,
She hasn't been kissed in forty years —
Hinky, dinky, parlez-vous.

O Madame, have you a daughter fine, parlez-vous?
O Madame, have you a daughter fine, parlez-vous?
O Madame, have you a daughter fine,
Fit for a soldier of the Line —
And his hinky pinky parlez-vous?

Oh yes, I have a daughter fine, parlez-vous,
Oh yes, I have a daughter fine, parlez-vous,
Oh yes, I have a daughter fine,
Fit for a soldier of the Line —
And his hinky pinky parlez-vous.

O Mademoiselle has eyes of brown, parlez-vous.
Her golden hair is hanging down, parlez-vous.
With her golden hair and her eyes of brown,

She's been kissed by all the troops in town —
And their hinky pinky parlez-vous.

The Colonel called on Mademoiselle, parlez-vous.
His carriage erect and his head as well, parlez-vous.
The Colonel called on Mademoiselle,
But she told him to go plump to hell —
With his hinky pinky parlez-vous.

A few of the innumerable verses of the popular First World War marching song.
Authorship is sometimes attributed to Gitz Rice, songwriter and composer and
original member of the Princess Pats, who maintained he transcribed a popular
French tune of 1915–16 and composed some verses and collected others. He
published a respectable version in 1919.

MADELON

There is a tavern way down in Brittany,
Where weary soldiers take their liberty.
The keeper's daughter, whose name is Madelon,
Pours out the wine while they laugh and carry on.
And while the wine goes to their senses,
Her sparkling glance goes to their hearts.
Their admiration so intense,
Each one his tale of love imparts.
She coquettes with them all but favours none at all.
And here's the way they banter every time they call.

Oh Madelon, you are the only one,
Oh Madelon, for you we'll carry on.
It's so long since we have seen a miss,
Won't you give us just a kiss?
But Madelon, she takes it all in fun,
She laughs and says, "I'll see it can't be done.
I would like but how can I consent
When I'm true to the whole regiment?"

First verse and chorus of "Madelon" as sung by the Princess Pats in France in
1918. The song was popular with French soldiers in 1914. The French words
were written by Louis Bousquet and the music composed by Camille Robert.
The English words are by Alfred Bryant.

A SONG OF WINTER WEATHER

ROBERT W. SERVICE

It isn't the foe that we fear;
It isn't the bullets that whine;
It isn't the business career
Of a shell, or the bust of a mine;
It isn't the snipers who seek
To nip our young hopes in the bud:
No, it isn't the guns,
And it isn't the Huns —
It's the mud,
    mud,
        mud.

It isn't the mêlée we mind.
That often is rather good fun.
It isn't the shrapnel we find
Obtrusive when rained by the ton;
It isn't the bounce of the bombs
That gives us a positive pain:
It's the strafing we get
When the weather is wet —
It's the rain,
    rain,
        rain.

It isn't because we lack grit
We shrink from the horrors of war.
We don't mind the battle a bit;
In fact that is what we are for;
It isn't the rum-jars and things
Make us wish we were back in the fold:
It's the fingers that freeze
In the boreal breeze —
It's the cold,
    cold,
        cold.

Oh, the rain, the mud, and the cold,
The cold, the mud, and the rain;
With weather at zero it's hard for a hero
From language that's rude to refrain.
With porridgy muck to the knees,
With sky that's a-pouring a flood,
Sure the worst of our foes
Are the pains and the woes
Of the *rain*,
      the *cold*,
           and the *mud*.

OUR DUG-OUT

EDGAR W. McINNIS

When the lines are in a muddle — as they very often are —
When the break's a mile away from you, or may be twice as far,
When you have to sort the trouble out, and fix it on the run,
It's fine to know that you can go, when everything is done,

To a cosy little dug-out (and the subject of this ode)
Just a comfy little bivvy on the —— Road,
A sheltered, sandbagged doorway with the flap flung open wide,
And a pal to grin a greeting when you step inside.

When the weather's simply damnable — cold sleet and driving
     rain —
When the poles snap off like matches and the lines are down
     again,
And you rip your freezing fingers as you work the stubborn wire,
It's great to get back home again, and dry off by the fire.

In a cheery little dug-out (and you know the kind I mean)
With a red-hot stove a-roaring, and a floor that's none too clean,
A pipe that's filled and waiting and a book that will not wait,
And a cup of steaming coffee if you come back late.

It may look a little crowded, and the roof's a trifle low,
But it's water-tight — or nearly — and it wasn't built for show,
And when Woolly Bears are crumping and the shrapnel sprays
    around,
You feel a whole lot safer if you're underneath the ground

In a rat-proof, rain-proof dug-out (and it's splinter-proof as well)
Where we got the stuff to build it is a thing I mustn't tell,
But we've made it strong and solid, and we're cosy, rain or shine,
In our happy little dug-out on the firing line.

THE PETROL TIN

W. P. JOHNSTON

I've read lots of rhymes of bully beef
And of beans of Simcoe brand;
Of plum and apples and old hard-tack,
And Maconock's stew so grand;
But ne'er a word have I ever heard,
And I think it is a sin,
So now I aim to write a line
About a petrol tin.

You'll find them round the dugouts,
Yes, anywhere in France;
We use 'em when we're standing still,
Also when in advance.
We use them in the old front line
For holding water in,
And I've seen them carry beer,
My boys, in a rusty petrol tin.

We use them in the cook-house —
Any cook can tell you that —
I've seen the boys a-playing cards
When on petrol tins they sat;
They're used for making mulligan,
Also for washing in;
Oh, what a life we all would have
But for a petrol tin!

We use them for a hundred things,
But I can't tell you all,
For the petrol tin I'm sitting on
Is just about to fall;
And I hear the bugles blowing,
So it's time that I begin
To get my stew and a drink of tea
That's made in a petrol tin.

A POT OF TEA

ROBERT W. SERVICE

You make it in your mess-tin by the brazier's rosy gleam;
You watch it cloud, then settle amber clear;
You lift it with your bay'nit, and you sniff the fragrant steam;
The very breath of it is ripe with cheer.
You're awful cold and dirty, and a-cursin' of your lot;
You scoff the blushin' 'alf of it, so rich and rippin' 'ot;
It bucks you up like anythink, just seems to touch the spot:
    God bless the man that first discovered Tea!

Since I came out to fight in France, which ain't the other day,
I think I've drunk enough to float a barge;
All kinds of fancy foreign dope, from caffy and doo lay,
To rum they serves you out before a charge.
In back rooms of estaminays I've gurgled pints of cham;

I've swilled down mugs of cider till I've felt a bloomin' dam;
But 'struth! they all ain't in it with the vintage of Assam:
   God bless the man that first invented Tea!

I think them lazy lumps o' gods wot kips on asphodel
Swigs nectar that's a flavour of Oolong;
I only wish them sons o' guns a-grillin' down in 'ell
Could 'ave their daily ration of Suchong.
Hurrah! I'm off to battle, which is 'ell and 'eaven too;
And if I don't give some poor bloke a sexton's job to do,
To-night, by Fritz's camp-fire, won't I 'ave a gorgeous brew
   (For fightin' mustn't interfere with Tea).
To-night we'll all be tellin' of the Boches that we slew,
   As we drink the giddy victory in Tea.

BALLAD OF BOOZE

LIEUTENANT JACK TURNER

Two extracts from Divisional Orders:
(1) Water from these wells to be drunk only after having been
chlorinated.
(2) An issue of Petrol tins (empty) has been authorized at the
rate of———per Bn. These cans will be used to hold drinking
water and will be shown as trench stores.

Bards sing the glory of the grape —
The sun-kissed clusters of the vine —
And claim some god in human shape
Brought down from heaven the gift of wine.
(I'd like to hear their Hymn of Hate
If they but had to sing their song
On luke-warm water taken straight
And chlorinated far too strong.)

Under the feet of maidens fair
Of old, 'tis said, the vintage flowed —
That was the stuff to banish care
And help a man along his road.
(How can a rhymester really rhyme,
Or scribble verses that will scan,
On water and chloride of lime,
Out of a rusty petrol can?)

Oh, shades of schooners that have sunk
Sailing across the polished bar!
Oh, dreams of all the drinks I've drunk,
Mem'ries of bottle, glass and jar!
Oh, Bacchus, veil thy vine-wreathed brow
And mourn the sorry fate of man:
I'm drinking muddy water now
Out of a rusty petrol can.

FROM THE TRENCHES

J. R. SMITH

I suppose we're a lot of heathens,
    Don't live on the Angel plan,
But we're sticking it here in the Trenches,
    And doing the best we can.

While preachers over in Canada,
    Who rave about Kingdom Come,
Ain't pleased with our ability,
    And are wanting to stop our rum.

Water, they say, would be better,
    Water, Great Scott! out here
We're up to our knees in water,
    Do they think we're standing in beer!

Oh, it sounds alright from the pulpit,
    When you sit in a cushion pew,
But try four days in the Trenches,
    And see how water will do.

They haven't the heart to say "thank you"
    For fighting on their behalf,
Perhaps they object to our smoking,
    Perhaps it's a fault to laugh.

Some of those toffee-faced blighters
    I think must be German bred,
It's time they called in a doctor
    For it's water they have in the head.

KEEP YOUR HEAD DOWN, FRITZI BOY

WORDS AND MUSIC BY GITZ RICE

Keep your head down, Fritzi boy,
Keep your head down, Fritzi boy.
Late last night
In the pale moon light
I saw you, I saw you.
You were fixing your barbed wire
When we opened rapid fire.
If you want to see your mother,
Your sister and your brother,
Keep your head down, Fritzi boy.

OF LICE AND SILK

TED PLANTOS

May 19, 1915

Families of lice
live in my uniform
and once every twenty-four hours,
they feed on my itching blood

The females lay eggs
in the seams and folds
where their families sleep
And every three days
the eggs hatch — twenty or so

Billy Rube wears
silk underclothes — says
they prevent infestation

The boys stopped laughing at Billy
after some set on fire
and others buried
their uniforms

But, though the world be dry and sad,
There are some places yet, methinks,
Where priests of Bacchus, linen-clad,
Concoct benign and soothing drinks.
Where men absorb the soothing rye,
Where highballs cheer the heart of man,
And the lone cherry floats on high —
Not in a rusty petrol can.

L'ENVOI

In vain, in vain, the grape may flow
From Leicester Square to Yucatan —
The only vintage that we know
Comes from a rusty petrol can.

BROTHER NEWT TO BROTHER FLY

PHILIP CHILD

Mysterious the twisted ways of men,
    Dear Brother Fly,
    And now and then
I marvel at the way the creatures die.
They perish joyfully to prove their soul —
    I wonder why?
Now I, had I a soul, should eat the whole
    Affair on earth;
Not love and kill and die so terribly
    To prove its worth.

Lo, yonder by the shattered German trench,
    A case in point —
    Ein kerker Mensch! —
The face (it's buried) has a bluish squint,
    And half a lip.
That he was *man* remains one only hint —
    That leg and hip.
It sticks there like an exclamation point
    That booted tip.

Mysterious the twisted ways of men,
    Dear Brother Fly,
    I marvel when
I see the curious way the creatures die:
A shell strikes, he erects that airy foot
    And so affirms
His soul is saved — and Germany to boot;
    So, glad to die.
Thank God we have no souls to justify,
    Let's dine on worms.

GOING OVER

MAJOR CHARLES G. D. ROBERTS

(The Somme 1917)

A girl's voice in the night troubled my heart.
Across the roar of the guns, the crash of the shells,
Low and soft as a sigh, clearly I heard it.

Where was the broken parapet, crumbling about me?
Where my shadowy comrades, crouching expectant?
A girl's voice in the dark troubled my heart.

A dream was the ooze of the trench, the wet clay slipping.
A dream the sudden out-flare of the wide-flung Verys.
I saw but a garden of lilacs, a-flower in the dusk.

What was the sergeant saying? — I passed it along. —
Did I pass it along? I was breathing the breath of the lilacs.
For a girl's voice in the night troubled my heart.

Over! How the mud sucks! Vomits red the barrage.
But I am far off in the hush of a garden of lilacs.
For a girl's voice in the night troubled my heart.
Tender and soft as a sigh, clearly I heard it.

WAR

ARTHUR STRINGER

From hill to hill he harried me;
    He stalked me day and night;
He neither knew nor hated me;
    Nor his nor mine the fight.

He killed the man who stood by me,
    For such they made his law;
Then foot by foot I fought to him,
    Who neither knew nor saw.

I trained my rifle on his heart;
    He leapt up in the air.
The screaming ball tore through his breast,
    And lay embedded there.

Lay hot embedded there, and yet
    Hissed home o'er hill and sea
Straight to the aching heart of one
    Who'd wronged not mine nor me!

I DIDN'T RAISE MY BOY TO BE A SOLDIER

ALFRED BRYAN

Ten million soldiers to the war have gone
Who may never return again,
Ten million hearts must break
For ones who died in vain.
Head bowed in sorrow, in her lonely years,
I heard a mother murmur through her tears:

I didn't raise my boy to be a soldier,
I brought him up to be my pride and joy.
Who dares to place a musket on his shoulder,
To shoot some other mother's darling boy?
Let nations arbitrate their future troubles,
It's time to lay the sword and gun away;
There'll be no war today, if mothers all would say,
I didn't raise my boy to be a soldier. . . .

What victory can cheer a mother's heart
When she looks at her blighted home?
What victory can bring her back
All she cared to call her own?
Let each mother answer in the years to be,
"Remember that my boy belongs to me."

This antiwar song was sung in 1915.

CAMBRAI AND MARNE

MAJOR CHARLES G. D. ROBERTS

(1914–1918)

Before our trenches at Cambrai
We saw their columns cringe away.
We saw their masses melt and reel
Before our line of leaping steel.

A handful to their storming hordes,
We scourged them with the scourge of swords,
And still, the more we slew, the more
Came up for every slain a score.

Between the hedges and the town
The cursing squadrons we rode down.
To stay them we outpoured our blood
Between the beetfields and the wood.

In that red hell of shrieking shell
Unfaltering our gunners fell;
They fell, or ere that day was done,
Beside the last unshattered gun.

But still we held them, like a wall
On which the breakers vainly fall —
Till came the word, and we obeyed,
Reluctant, bleeding, undismayed.

Our feet, astonished, learned retreat;
Our souls rejected, still, defeat.
Unbroken still, a lion at bay,
We drew back grimly from Cambrai.

In blood and sweat, with slaughter spent,
They thought us beaten as we went;
Till suddenly we turned and smote
The shout of triumph in their throat.

At last, at last we turned and stood —
And Marne's fair water ran with blood;
We stood by trench and steel and gun,
For now the indignant flight was done.

We ploughed their shaken ranks with fire,
We trod their masses into mire.
Our sabres drove through their retreat,
As drives the whirlwind through young wheat.

At last, at last we drove them back
Along their drenched and smoking track.
We hurled them back, in blood and flame,
The reeking ways by which they came.

By cumbered road and desperate ford,
How fled their shamed and harassed horde!
Shout, Sons of Freemen, for the day
When Marne so well avenged Cambrai!

GAS CLOUDS

TED PLANTOS

April 22, 1915

Tommy Morgan
pisses
in his handkerchief,
holds it to his face
I waste no time doing the same when I see my comrades
falling,
mouths filled with a strange metal
taste — froth
shrieking
at their lips
and the backs of their throats
hooked
and torn
by nausea

I cannot see through the fumes
and smoke
while the Germans
advance, gas-masked
through the clouds
now thinning with our lives
to a vapour

THE THIRD BATTLE OF YPRES

RAYMOND SOUSTER

My old man dropped his piece of bread
in the Passchendaele mud, picked it up
again, wiped it off a little

and ate it. He stood in the water
to his waist at the guns
and stopped only long enough from loading
to watch a fellow gunner
spin round three times before he fell
with his head blown off.
A shirt my mother sent him
he wore three weeks
without changing it.
Finally it walked off his back.

None of this has ever
become part of history, which is
battles and generals. Well, those generals
tried hard enough to kill my father,
but he somehow escaped them.
                    Still, if he lives
a few years longer they may get him yet.

YPRES

BRUCE MEYER

The London Times reported
That men had seen St. George
Battling with grey shell bursts
High above the field.

Some ignored the figures
As trench fatigue.
Others thought of rain
Turning the ground to mud.

In trenches named Death's Alley
Hell Row and Devil's Way
They watched the bombardment flicker,
Stagelights for the opening act.

Onslaught came
Rolling yellow clouds
Like mill smoke
Toward the lines.

The African colonials fled
Ran barefoot as the mustard gas
Made angels and barbed wire
Disappear in blindness.

Ross rifles jammed on ammunition
And those that fired became red hot.
The only weapons of defence:
Bayonets, or clubs, or rocks.

It was not an English Saint they saw
But ghosts of Dollard and Lundy's Lane.
A hagiology born in mud
Where earth took communion with the sky.

YPRES: 1915

ALDEN NOWLAN

The age of trumpets is passed, the banners hang
like dead crows, tattered and black,
rotting into nothingness on cathedral walls.
In the crypt of St. Paul's I had all the wrong thoughts,
wondered if there was anything left of Nelson
or Wellington, and even wished
I could pry open their tombs and look,
then was ashamed
of such morbid childishness, and almost afraid.

I know the picture is as much a forgery
as the Protocols of Zion, yet it outdistances

more plausible fictions: newsreels, regimental histories,
biographies of Earl Haig.
                              It is always morning
and the sky somehow manages to be red
though the picture is in black and white.
There is a long road over flat country,
shell holes, the debris of houses,
a gun carriage overturned in a field,
the bodies of men and horses,
but only a few of them and those
always neat and distant.
                              The Moors are running
down the right side of the road.
The Moors are running
in their baggy pants and Santa Claus caps.
The Moors are running.
                              And their officers,
Frenchmen who remember
Alsace and Lorraine,
are running backwards in front of them,
waving their swords, trying to drive them back,
weeping
            at the dishonour of it all.
The Moors are running.

And on the left side of the same road,
the Canadians are marching
in the opposite direction.

The Canadians are marching
in English uniforms behind
a piper playing "Scotland the Brave."

The Canadians are marching
in impeccable formation,
every man in step.

The Canadians are marching.

And I know this belongs
with Lord Kitchener's mustache
and old movies in which the Kaiser and his general staff
seem to run like the Keystone Kops.

That old man on television last night,
a farmer or fisherman by the sound of him,
revisiting Vimy Ridge, and they asked him
what it was like, and he said,
There was water up to our middles, yes
and there was rats, and yes
there was water up to our middles
and rats, all right enough,
and to tell you the truth
after the first three or four days
I started to get a little disgusted.

Oh, I know they were mercenaries
in a war that hardly concerned us.
I know all that.

Sometimes I'm not even sure that I have a country.

But I know they stood there at Ypres
the first time the Germans used gas,
that they were almost the only troops
in that section of the front
who did not break and run,
who held the line.

Perhaps they were too scared to run.
Perhaps they didn't know any better
— that is possible, they were so innocent,
those farmboys and mechanics, you have only to look
at old pictures and see how they smiled.
Perhaps they were too shy
to walk out on anybody, even Death.
Perhaps their only motivation
was a stubborn disinclination.

Private MacNally thinking:
You squareheaded sons of bitches,
you want this God damn trench
you're going to have to take it away
from Billy MacNally
of the South End of Saint John, New Brunswick.

And that's ridiculous, too, and nothing
on which to found a country.
                                        Still
It makes me feel good, knowing
that in some obscure, conclusive way
they were connected with me
and me with them.

PASSCHENDAELE, OCTOBER 1917

RAYMOND SOUSTER

Half-drowning in the miserable lean-to
that was really just a tin roof over mud,
my father heard a strange plop plop plop
almost on top of him, panicked, yelled at Fred
who was drowsing beside him,
and with both hands shaking
somehow pulled his gas-mask on.

But old Fred wasn't buying it this time,
he was sick to death of false alarms,
so didn't budge until the first yellow cloud
seeped in a minute later (my father watching
through his half-fogged goggles, hear Fred cough,
then struggle with his gas-mask,
cough, clutch his throat again,
then jump up, scramble out, a madman screaming
as he ran for the battery gas-curtain . . .).

Six months or so later he was back,
his lungs almost good as new.

TO A CANADIAN AVIATOR WHO DIED FOR HIS COUNTRY IN FRANCE

DUNCAN CAMPBELL SCOTT

Tossed like a falcon from the hunter's wrist,
A sweeping plunge, a sudden shattering noise,
And thou has dared, with a long spiral twist,
The elastic stairway to the rising sun,
Peril below thee and above, peril
Within thy ear; but peril cannot daunt
Thy peerless heart: gathering wing and poise,
Thy plane transfigured, and thy motor-chant
Subduèd to a whisper — then a silence, —
And thou are but a disembodied venture
In the void.

But Death, who has learned to fly,
Still matchless when his work is to be done,
Met thee between the armies and the sun;
Thy speck of shadow faltered in the sky;
Then thy dead engine and thy broken wings
Drooped through the arc and passed in fire,
A wreath of smoke — a breathless exhalation.
But ere that came a vision sealed thine eyes,
Lulling thy senses with oblivion;
And from its sliding station in the skies
Thy dauntless soul upward in circles soared
To the sublime and purest radiance where it sprang.

In all their eyries, eagles shall mourn thy fate,
And leaving on the lonely crags and scaurs
Their unprotected young, shall congregate
High in the tenuous heaven and anger the sun
With screams, and with a wild audacity
Dare all the battle danger of thy flight;
Till weary with combat one shall desert the light,

Fall like a bolt of thunder and check his fall
On the high ledge, smoky with mist and cloud,
Where his neglected eaglets shriek aloud,
And drawing the film across his sovereign sight
Shall dream of thy swift soul immortal
Mounting in circles, faithful beyond death.

THE AVENGING ANGEL

WILFRED CAMPBELL

(To Flight Lieutenant Robinson and all the heroic aviators of the Royal Flying Corps)

When the last faint red of the day is dead,
    And the dim, far heaven is lit
        With the silvern oars
        Of the orient stars,
    And the winged winds whimper and flit;

Then I rise through the dome of my aerodrome,
    Like a giant eagle in flight;
        And I take my place
        In the vengeful race
    With the sinister fleets of night.

As I rise and rise in the cloudy skies,
    No sound in the silence is heard,
        Save the lonesome whirr
        Of my engine's purr,
    Like the wings of a monster bird.

And naught is seen save the vault, serene,
    Of the vasty realms of night,
        That vanish, aloof,
        To eternity's roof,
    As I mount in my ominous flight.

And I float and pause in the fleecy gauze,
   Like a bird in a nest of down;
     While 'neath me in deeps
     Of blackness, sleeps
   The far, vast London town.

But I am not here, like a silvern sphere,
   To glory the deeps of space,
     But a sentinel, I,
     In this tower of the sky,
   Scanning the dim deep's face.

For, sudden, afar, like a luminous star,
   Or a golden horn of the moon,
     Or a yellow leaf
     Of the forest's grief,
   When the autumn winds are atune;

There is borne on my sight, down the spaces of night,
   By the engines of evilment sped,
     That wonderful, rare,
     Vast ship of the air,
   Beautiful, ominous, dread.

One instant she floats, most magic of boats,
   Illusive, implacable, there;
     Throned angel of ill,
     On her crystal-built hill,
   O'er a people's defenceless despair.

Then sudden, I rise, like a bolt through the skies,
   To the very dim roofs of the world;
     Till down in the grey,
     I see my grim prey,
   Like a pallid gold leaf, upcurled.

And I hover and swing, until swiftly I spring,
  And drop like a falling star;
    And again and again,
    My death-dealing rain,
  Hurl to the deeps afar.

Then I hover and listen, till I see the far glisten
  Of a flame-flash blanching the night;
    And I know that my hate,
    That has lain in wait,
  Has won in the grim air-fight.

Then I curve and slant, while my engines pant,
  And the wings of my great bird tame;
    While the sinister Hun,
    In his ill, undone,
  Goes out in a blinding flame.

OUR WOMEN

L. M. MONTGOMERY

Bride of a day, your eye is bright,
  And the flower of your cheek is red.
'He died with a smile on a field of France —
  I smile for his sake,' she said.

Mother of one, the babe you bore
  Sleeps in a chilly bed.
'He gave himself with a gallant pride —
  Shall I be less proud?' she said.

Woman, you weep and sit apart,
  Whence is your sorrow fed?
'I have none of love or kin to go —
  I am shamed and sad,' she said.

WAR MUSIC: RATIONING

NURSE DAISY COOK

Music flows through many words.
Here are five so soft and gay,
Sweeter than the songs of birds:
"Coupon Ten is good today."

THE GIRL BEHIND THE MAN BEHIND THE GUN

WILSON MACDONALD

You have seen the line of khaki swinging grandly down the
    street;
    You have heard the band blare out Brittanic songs:
You have read a ton of papers and you've thrown them at your
    feet,
    And your brain's a battlefield for fighting throngs.
You have cheered for Tommy Atkins and you've yelled for Jack
    Canuck;
    You have praised the French and Belgians, every one;
But I'm rhyming here a measure to the valour and the pluck
    Of the Girl behind the Man behind the Gun.

There's a harder game than fighting, there's a deeper wound by
    far
    Than the bayonet or the bullet ever tore;
And a patient little woman wears upon her heart a scar
    Which the lonesome years will keep for evermore.
There are bands and bugles crying and the horses madly ride,
    And in passion are the trenches lost or won;
But SHE battles in the silence with no comrade at her side —
    Does the Girl behind the Man behind the Gun.

They are singing songs in Flanders and there's music on the
    wind,
    They are shouting for their country and their king;
But the hallways yearn for music in the homes they left behind,
    For the mother of a soldier does not sing.
In the silence of the night-time, 'mid a ring of hidden foes,
    And without a bugle cry to cheer her on,
She is fighting fiercer battles than a soldier ever knows
    And her triumph — is an open grave, at dawn.

You have cheered the line of khaki swinging grandly down the
    street,
    But you quite forgot to cheer another line;
They are plodding sadly homeward, with no music for their feet,
    To a far more lonely river than the Rhine.
Ah! the battlefield is wider than the cannon's sullen roar,
    And the women weep o'er battles lost or won;
For the man — a cross of honour, but the crepe upon the door
    For the Girl behind the Man behind the Gun.

When the heroes are returning and the world with flags is red,
    When you show the tattered trophies of the war,
When your cheers are for the living, and your tears are for the
    dead
    Which the foemen in the battle trampled o'er,
When you fling your reddest roses at the horsemen in array
    With their helmets flaming proudly in the sun,
I would bid you wear the favour of an apple-blossom spray
    For the Girl behind the Man behind the Gun.

K-K-K-KATY

GEOFFREY O'HARA

Jimmy was a soldier brave and bold,
Katy was a maid with hair of gold,
Like an act of fate,
Kate was standing at the gate,
Watching all the boys on dress parade.

Jimmy with the girls was just a gawk,
Stuttered every time he tried to talk,
Still that night at eight,
He was there at Katy's gate,
Stuttering to her this love-sick cry.

K-K-K-Katy, beautiful Katy,
You're the only g-g-g-girl that I adore;
When the m-moon shines,
Over the cow-shed,
I'll be waiting at the k-k-k-kitchen door!

No one ever looked so nice and neat,
No one could be just as cute and sweet,
That's what Jimmy thought,
When the wedding ring he bought,
Now he's off to France the foe to meet.

Jimmy thought he'd like to take a chance,
See if he could make the Kaiser dance,
Stepping to a tune,
All about the silvery moon,
This is what they hear in far-off France.

K-K-K-Katy, beautiful Katy,
You're the only g-g-g-girl that I adore;
When the m-moon shines,
Over the cow-shed,
I'll be waiting at the k-k-k-kitchen door.

IN FLANDERS FIELDS

JOHN McCRAE

In Flanders fields the poppies blow
Between the crosses, row on row,
   That mark our place; and in the sky
   The larks, still bravely singing, fly
Scarce heard amid the guns below.

We are the Dead. Short days ago
We lived, felt dawn, saw sunset glow,
   Loved and were loved, and now we lie
   In Flanders fields.

Take up our quarrel with the foe:
To you from failing hands we throw
   The torch; be yours to hold it high.
   If ye break faith with us who die
We shall not sleep, though poppies grow
   In Flanders fields.

IN FLANDERS NOW

EDNA JAQUES

We have kept faith, ye Flanders' dead,
   Sleep well beneath those poppies red
That mark your place.
The torch your dying hands did throw,
   We've held it high before the foe,
And answered bitter blow for blow,
   In Flanders' fields.

And where your heroes' blood was spilled,
   The guns are now forever stilled
And silent grown.

There is no moaning of the slain,
  There is no cry of tortured pain,
And blood will never flow again,
  In Flanders' fields.

Forever holy in our sight
  Shall be those crosses gleaming white,
That guard your sleep.
Rest you in peace, the task is done,
  The fight you left us we have won,
And Peace on Earth has just begun,
  In Flanders now.

THE VIMY MEMORIAL
(for April 9, 1917)

WATSON KIRKCONNELL

(Elegiac couplets)

High on the summit it towers and gazes in silence to eastward,
  Over the plain of Douai, over the lowlands of France:
Based on twin ramparts of ashlars, upreared in a pile cyclopean,
  Flanked with cold figures of stone, worthy of Mizraim's
    prime,
Pillars of marble upsoaring, stupendous and touched with the
    sunrise,
  Speak of a battle of old, tell of a victory won.

Yonder to westward, far down, in the sheltering shades of the
    valley,
  Deep in the dark of the night, low in the slush of the spring,
Stirred a conspiring army of wakeful Canadian legions,
  Poised for the word of command, tense for the shout of
    attack.

Sudden the thunder of guns tore asunder the mists of the
     morning,
     Full in the face of the foe, first on the front of their line,
Then with relentless precision it swept the impregnable hillside,
     Rending its trenches to mud, churning its nests into shreds.
Back of that creeping barrage four divisions came shoulder to
     shoulder,
     Every man's bayonet fixed, every man's magazine filled,
Smashing the outermost hinge of the enemy's mighty
     emplacement,
     Storming the obstinate ridge, held through two years of
     despair.
Slopes were a slither of slush and a chaos of shell-smitten
     ramparts,
     Enemy fire was fierce, taking a terrible toll;
Thousands of khaki-clad figures lay dead in the wake of the
     onset;
     Thousands of field-grey foes littered the hillside in death.
Less than an hour was to pass till the troops of the foremost
     Dominion
     Stood on the crest of the hill, gazed in grim joy to the plain.
Here stands the noble Memorial, marking the place of their
     triumph;
     This was their greatest deed, this their most notable hour.
Here amid warfare titanic, and armies that massed in their
     millions,
     One great Canadian Corps moved as one man to its goal.
There had been bloodier slaughter of soldiers at Ypres and
     Givenchy,
     Bloodier still on the Somme, murder in oceans of mud,
Capturing water-clogged shell-holes and wreckage of derelict
     hamlets,

     Churning up cauldrons of clay, pouring in life-blood of men.
Climax of all of the pain was to come at the close of October —
     Thrown into Passchendaele's slough, countless Canadians
     died.
Months of incessant bombardment had shattered the
     countryside's drainage;

Autumn's torrential rains had formed an impassable bog;
Guns were to sink to the axle, the artillery horse to his belly;
Men were like clotted flies, caught in the glutinous ooze.
Generals, British and French, in their rivalry only for fame,
Poured out the lives of their men, setting impossible tasks.
Borden and Currie made protest, and threats to withdraw from the contest
Rather than lose of their best, slain at a field-marshal's whim.
Amiens yet was to come, and Arras and Cambrai thereafter,
Victory followed at last, victory bought with a price.

Here on the hilltop at Vimy the monument stands in remembrance;
Threescore thousand dead, these were the price that we paid.
Here will their spirits foregather, pale ghosts of our nearest and dearest,
Thronging the steps of the plinth, thronging the platform of stone.
What will they dream as released from the clogging constraint of the body
Over the flatlands they gaze, over the lowlands of France?
Will they rehearse all the battles that raged on those plains through the ages —
Caesar assailing the Gauls, Attila's army of Huns,
Saracens sweeping in ardour to conquer the world for the Crescent,
Norsemen who land from their ships, feudal despite to the Crown,
All of the sweep of the warfare that followed the French Revolution,
Legions from over the Rhine, brought by the French on themselves?

Such may the reveries be of the ghosts of our kinsmen departed:
Deeds of a handful of dust, vanquishing valorous dust.
Will they be proud as they see, in our land that they laid down their lives for,
Petty political spite, bickering selfish and crude?

Deathless their valour remains, to rebuke the small souls who
    come after.
If we should founder in shame, ghosts of our great will be
    grieved.

VIMY UNVEILING

JOE WALLACE

How strange that grass
Should rise so green
From rains that fall
So red.

FOYE BUCKNER OF HAINESVILLE, NEW BRUNSWICK, RECALLS HIS SERVICE WITH THE CONNAUGHT LIGHT INFANTRY 1914–1918

ALDEN NOWLAN

They told us afterwards we'd been in France;
hell take that place, it rained continually.
The Northrup girl who hears but cannot speak
squawks like a German and as shamelessly.

London was where we vomited, the beer
warmer than piss, the girls like carpeting;
and once, astonished that he looked so small
on his high balcony, I saw the king.

TWO CANADIAN MEMORIALS

I

We giving all gained all.
  Neither lament us nor praise.
Only in all things recall,
  It is Fear, not Death that slays.

II

From little towns in a far land we came,
  To save our honour and a world aflame.
By little towns in a far land we sleep;
  And trust that world we won for you to keep!

Rudyard Kipling composed these "Epitaphs of the War: 1914–18" for
cenotaphs in Sudbury and Sault Ste. Marie respectively.

MEMORIAL CHAMBER INSCRIPTION

THEY ARE TOO NEAR TO BE GREAT
BUT OUR CHILDREN SHALL UNDERSTAND
WHEN AND HOW OUR FATE WAS CHANGED
AND BY WHOSE HAND

These lines, composed by Rudyard Kipling, were engraved on a stone tablet and
erected in the Memorial Chamber of the Peace Tower of the Parliament
Buildings in Ottawa, only to be removed in 1982.

13

THE SPANISH CIVIL WAR

The Spanish Civil War has been called the bloodiest and noblest civil war of all time. The military revolt against the Republican government of Spain broke out on July 17, 1936. The Nationalist rebels, led by General Francisco Franco, were supported by conservative elements within the country and aided by Fascist Italy and Nazi Germany. The Republican government was assisted by the Soviet Union and by volunteers from many countries.

The number of Canadians who volunteered to serve the Republican cause was 1,239. In July 1937, they formed the Mackenzie-Papineau Battalion of the XVth International Brigade of the Spanish Republican Army, and they fought valiantly at Jarama, Quinto, Belchite, Teruel, and the Ebro. The novelist Hugh Garner was among their number. Dr. Norman Bethune at Madrid mounted the world's first mobile blood-transfusion service. The war effectively ended with the Nationalists entering Madrid on March 28, 1939.

Since it was a criminal offence for any Canadian citizen to enlist in a foreign army, official records were not kept of the Canadian involvement in the Spanish Civil War. It is known that 385 Canadian soldiers were killed in Spain; the number is probably higher, as the fate of many others remains obscure. Some of the volunteers who returned did so with difficulty, as the RCMP tried to bar their re-entry. They are unhonoured in the battle records of the country to this day.

BATTLE HYMN OF THE SPANISH REBELLION

L. A. MACKAY

The Church's one foundation
    Is now the Moslem sword,
In meek collaboration
    With flame, and axe, and cord;
While overhead are floating,
    Deep-winged with holy love,
The battle planes of Wotan,
    The bombing planes of Jove.

TO ONE GONE TO THE WARS

A. M. KLEIN

For S.H.A.

Unworthiest crony of my grammar days,
    Expectorator in learning's cuspidor,
Forsaking the scholar's for the gamin's ways,
    The gates of knowledge for the cubicular door,

How you have shamed me, me the noble talker,
    The polisher of phrases, stainer of verbs,
Who daily for a price serve hind and hawker,
    Earning my Sabbath meat, my daily herbs.

'Tis you who do confound the lupine jaw
    And stand protective of my days and works,
As in the street-fight you maintain the law
    And I in an armchair — weigh and measure Marx.

Alas, that fettered and bound by virtues long since rusty,
I must, for spouse and son,
Withhold, as is befitting any prison trusty,
My personal succour and my uniformed aid,
And from the barracks watch the barricade —
Offering you, meek sacrifice, unvaliant gift,
My non-liturgic prayer:
For that your aim be sure,
Your bullet swift
Unperilous your air, your trenches dry,
Your courage unattainted by defeat,
Your courage high.

SPAIN

DOROTHY LIVESAY

When the bare branch responds to leaf and light
Remember them: it is for this they fight.
It is for haze-swept hills and the green thrust
Of pine, that they lie choked with battle dust.

You who hold beauty at your finger-tips
Hold it because the splintering gunshot rips
Between your comrades' eyes; hold it across
Their bodies' barricade of blood and loss.

You who live quietly in sunlit space
Reading The Herald after morning grace
Can count peace dear, when it has driven
Your sons to struggle for this grim, new heaven.

RED MOON

NORMAN BETHUNE

And this same pallid moon tonight,
　Which rides so quietly, clear and high,
The mirror of our pale and troubled gaze,
　Raised to a cool Canadian sky,

Above the shattered Spanish mountain tops
　Last night, rose low and wild and red,
Reflecting back from her illumined shield,
　The blood-bespattered faces of the dead.

To that pale disc we raise our clenched fists
　And to those nameless dead, our vows renew,
"Comrades, who fought for freedom and the future world
　Who died for us, we will remember you."

I COME FROM CUATRO CAMINOS

I come from Cuatro Caminos,
From Cuatro Caminos I come,
My eyes are overflowing,
And clouded with blood.
The blood of a little fair one,
Whom I saw destroyed on the ground;
The blood of a young woman,
The blood of an old man, a very old man,
The blood of many people, of many
Trusting, helpless,
Fallen under the bombs
Of the pirates of the air.
I come from Cuatro Caminos,

From Cuatro Caminos I come,
My ears are deaf
With blasphemies and wailings,
Ay Little One, Little One;
What hast thou done to these dogs
That they have dashed thee in pieces
On the stones of the grounds?
Ay, ay, ay, Mother, my Mother;
Why have they killed the old grandfather?
Because they are wolf's cubs,
Cubs of a man-eating wolf.
Because the blood that runs in their veins
Is blood of brothel and mud
Because in their regiment
They were born fatherless
A "curse on God" rends the air
Towards the infamy of Heaven.

Norman Bethune was inspired to write this poem by the bombing of a hospital at Cuatro Caminos. "A working-class residential area of Madrid, Cuatro Caminos was a constant target for savage aerial attacks by Nationalist bombers," according to Roderick Stewart.

OUR MORNING STAR

We have a man triumphant over death,
Lift up your hearts, for we have Comrade Beth!
Doctor Bethune who died for us afar
Who is our glory and our morning star,
Our grief, our glory, and our morning star.

These lines (the concluding ones from "The Saga of Doctor Bethune" by Joe Wallace) were written in memory of Norman Bethune, who served as a medical doctor in Spain and died in China in 1939, having joined the Eighth Route Army of the Chinese Communists.

14

THE SECOND
WORLD WAR

The Parliament of Canada declared, on September 10, 1939, that a state of war existed between Germany and Canada. The Canadian declaration followed that of Britain by seven days. It was not until December 1941 that the United States formally entered the war.

Canadian participation in the Second World War marked the greatest collective effort of the Canadian people. It transformed an agricultural nation into an industrial one. Although overseas service was voluntary until 1944, opinion in the country was polarized on the subject of conscription. The war economy touched the life of each and every citizen. A total of 730,625 Canadians saw service with the Canadian Army, the Royal Canadian Navy, and the Royal Canadian Air Force. A total of 41,992 servicemen and -women lost their lives before the German surrender was taken on May 8, 1945, and the Japanese surrender on September 2, 1945.

Canadian soldiers saw action on many fronts. Sites of some of the principal Canadian engagements include Agira, Arnhem, Bayeux, Boulogne, Caen, Calais, Dieppe, Falaise, Hochwald Ridge, Hong Kong, Kapelsche Veer, Le Havre, Messina, Nijmegen, Normandy, Ortona, Reichswald, Rhine, Scheldt, Spitsbergen, and Vierrères Ridge. The dark of the Dieppe raid of August 19, 1942, contrasted with the light of the Normandy invasion of June 6, 1944.

The poems, songs, and verses of the Second World War are arranged more or less chronologically but with a division into services — Army, Navy, Air Force. Many powerful poems and songs were written by combatants and observers, though none caught the public's heart as much as "In Flanders Fields" did in the First World War. Probably the most-remembered poem occasioned by the Second World War is "High Flight." The sonnet was written by Pilot Officer John Gillespie Magee, Jr. (1922–41), a young American who left Yale University to enlist with the Royal Canadian Air Force in Montreal in September 1940. He served overseas with a Spitfire squadron of the Royal Air Force and was killed in action on December 11, 1941. He wrote "High Flight" on the back of a letter addressed to his mother three months before his tragic death. It was chosen as the official poem of the RAF and the RCAF and posted in pilot-training centres throughout the Commonwealth. It captures the excitement of aerial navigation.

CREED

DICK DIESPECKER

If they should ask you,
Why do you fight?
Tell them, For Freedom. For the right
To live in peace; to worship God;
To build a cottage, turn a sod
That is my own; to trust my friends;
To know that when the work day ends,
A wife and children wait to greet
Me with a smile. I fight to meet
The future unashamed; to read
What books I will; to choose the creed
I wish; face politicians unafraid,
And criticize, if need be, laws they've made.
These are the web of life; for these I lend
My strength; these are the rights that I defend.

ARMY

IN TIME OF WAR

DOROTHY LIVESAY

(Excerpt)

You went, wordless; but I had not the will
Nor courage to find fanciful or plumaged phrase
To camouflage my solitude. So saying bald
Good-bye, word bouncing down each waiting step
Till out of sight and sound, I saw you turn
Walk firm toward the iron gate. Its clang
Shattered a world. For should we greet again
This hushed horizon will have widened so
You'll not find solace walking in the Park
Or watching storm snarl over English Bay.
That night of fog, bleaching the bones of trees
Will not shroud you and me again; too wide apart
We will have grown; our thoughts too proud
Too tall for sheltering beneath these boughs.

ON GOING TO THE WARS

EARLE BIRNEY

I do not go, my dear, to storm
The praise of men; this uniform
May shine less gay in gas and mud
And be medallioned but by blood,
While lips that know your lips will turn
Uneasily to harlot worm.
And war, it's true, fouls both the flesh
Victorious and the flesh it slays.

Yet must we play the beast afresh
To claw from wolves their power to craze
The heirs of Raphael and the kin
Of Bach, our friends the foe.
I, too, let's say, a travail owe:
So that our son, who curls within
The womb, may wake to brighter earth,
I must not shrink from giving birth
To death.
      I go that he may stare
Blue-eyed into Canadian air
Unhaunted by the charnel birds
That drop their excrement of death.
I go that he may draw free breath
To speak the rich and ancient words
We use, and spell from books unburned,
And teachers not from trueness turned.
I march that he may learn from grass
And rose what we have missed, the pass
To quiet life, and never set
The rendezvous my father met
In vain.
      I go that we may breast
Again the Dorset downs in zest
And walk the Kentish lanes where I
Began a larger life in knowing
You. Yet if from seething sky
I win reprieve but by the slowing
Crutch, or whitened cane, my doom
Will yet have helped to hold in bloom
Old English orchards and Canadian
Woods unscarred by steel, Acadian
And Columbian roofs unswept
By flame. My mother will be kept
From stumbling down a prairie road
Illumed by burning barns and snowed
By patterned death.
      Is it so rash

To seek to rank with men who saved
Your English father from a lash
In London streets, and bent head shaved
Because his mother was a Jew
Who starved last year in Lodz? And you —
My dear, I'll not survive to see
You bricked within a ghetto slum
In Canada, by booted scum.
I pledge that if by chance I flee
The blundering malice of the guns
I'll stand by those who strive to chart
A world where peace is everyone's,
A peace that does not rot the heart
With hunger, fear, and hopeless hate,
Nor rust the cunning wheels nor still
The subtle fingers, peace that will
Unlock to every man the gate
To all the leaping joys his hand
Creates. For no less prize I stand.

And now, my dear, since we may yet
Delight in leaf uncrinkling, and
In maple woods the violet,
Then let us from the patient land
Take strength, nor fail to share the charmed
Routine of stars, or trysting keep
With common things, with evenings warmed
By music, food, and love, and sleep.

For present solace these, but for
Our hope we've nowhere else to look
Except into our spirit's book.
No hell unspilled by lords of war
Upon the people's flesh has ever
Parched the human heart's endeavour,
The human will to love and truth.
For one face mired in black unruth
A score will signal us each day
The sun unquenched within our clay.

Across the tundra of our dread
We must beat on, windbitten, to
The unseen cabin's light, and through
The glooming western firwoods thread,
In hope to pass the peaks terrific,
And win the wide sundrenched Pacific.

THE SECOND WORLD WAR

MILTON ACORN

Down Great George Street, up to the station;
The skirl of the pipes the very thrill of your nerves
With the pipemaster (only man who has the Gaelic)
Ahead with his great baton, his strut and toss proud
        as any man who's ever walked.
This is where we came in; this has happened before
Only the last time there was cheering.
So few came back they changed the name of the regiment
So there're no cheers now. Tho there are crowds
Standing silent, eyes wide as dolls' eyes, but brighter
Trying to memorize every face

This is where we came in. It happened before.
        The last time was foolishness
Now's got to be done because of the last foolishness.
In the ranks, perfectly in step (with the pipes
        even I'm perfectly in step)
I'm thinking of Through the Looking Glass:
The White King's armies marching while he sleeps;
We are his dream. . . . At least it seems that way.
They're so clumsy the front line topples
The second line topples over it; and on it goes
        — line after line, eyes glazed straight forward
Shoulders back, spines held stiffly unnatural
Toppling over the line before

So few came back they abolished the regiment.
I was lucky — sickness and bad marksmanship.
Man by man we'd sworn to take our guns back,
    man by man we didn't.
One man — one war — that's all he's usually good for.
Now a strange short-haired subculture
Glares at us out of the TV set
Snarling the news, every phrase or disguised opinion
    as if it was a threat, which it is.
This is where we came in
It's happened before.
This last time was right
But ended in foolishness.
It has happened before, could happen again
Despite the fact that stuff is out of date.

RECRUIT

DOUGLAS LOCHHEAD

You will sign here.

You will understand
    that this is the army,
    that there is an enemy somewhere
    and that social disease
    is where you find it.

You will about turn
    counting three, placing
    the left foot slightly at an angle.
You will salute all college boys
    and sons of merchants
    raising the right arm . . .

You will breathe slowly twice
   kissing the stock with right cheek
   before squeezing trigger.
You will remember the Bren weighs
   twenty-six and one half pounds.
   To change the barrel simply . . .

You will see that darkness is not always
   for love, but patrols,
   planned nightmares, where arms are words
   and the enemy a past-master.

You will write "X" in squares
   meaning for mothers, your heart
   is pure, and the socks fit well,
   and please send more cigarettes.

You will recognize the mortar's womp
   without holler, never digging
   your glory hole below trees
   whose branches catch strange birds
   in their hair.

You will listen to all men
   wearing ribbons.
You will listen to those
   who have seen the glory.

You will pray when no one is looking.
You will curl in fear, in the womb
   of your pounding blood,
   in your private bed of whittled thorns.

ABOUT BEING A MEMBER
OF OUR ARMED FORCES

AL PURDY

Remember the early days of the phony war
when men were zombies and women were CWACS
and they used wooden rifles on the firing range?
Well I was the sort of soldier you couldn't trust
with a wooden rifle
and when they gave me a wooden bayonet
life was fraught with peril for my brave comrades
including the sergeant-instructor
I wasn't exactly a soldier tho
        only a humble airman
who kept getting demoted and demoted and demoted
to the point where I finally saluted civilians
And when they trustingly gave me a Sten gun
Vancouver should have trembled in its sleep
for after I fired a whole clip of bullets
at some wild ducks under Burrard Bridge
(on guard duty at midnight)
they didn't fly away for five minutes
trying to decide if there was any danger
Not that the war was funny
I took it and myself quite seriously
the way a squirrel in a treadmill does
too close to tears for tragedy
too far from the banana peel for laughter
and I didn't blame anyone for being there
that wars happened wasn't anybody's fault then
now I think it is

Canadian Women's Army Corps

ANONYMOUS

1. VICTORY LOAN POEM

You can back the attack by dating a CWAC,
Press your suit — get a haircut and shave.
Just stroll hand in hand, through the snow or the sand,
And buy bonds with the dough you both save.

2. SABOTAGED VERSION

Don't back the attack by dating a CWAC,
Though its tempting — you still must be brave.
Take a last lingering look, go home, read a book,
And buy bonds with the money you save.

WAVE

ANONYMOUS

His wife was a WAVE and he waved at a CWAC;
The CWAC was in front, his WAVE was in back.
Instead of a wave from the CWAC, be it said,
He won but a whack from the WAVE he had wed.

WILLIE THE LION

RAYMOND SOUSTER

Mackenzie King said
"Conscription if necessary
but not necessarily conscription. . . ."

(So they took Steve in England,
gave him one whole week
of infantry refresher
and shipped him across
to the Hochwald where
after three nightmare days
of living on rum
an S.S. mortar
blew his left side off)

the historians say
Mr. King saved Canada

as for Steve —
he gets a pension
can walk with a cane

Zombies

ANONYMOUS

1. SEVENTY THOUSAND ZOMBIES

Seventy thousand Zombies,
Isn't it a farce,
Seventy thousand Zombies,
Sitting on their -----?
Eating up the rations,
Morning, noon and night,
Squatting here in Canada,
While others go to fight.

Seventy thousand Zombies,
Hear the bastards sing,
"Here's our thanks to you, Quebec,
And old Mackenzie King.

Never mind our comrades,
Let them be the goats,
As long as politicians
Protect their slimy votes."

Seventy thousand Zombies,
Refuse to play their game,
God, our fair Dominion,
Must hang its head in shame.
"Recruits are badly needed,"
You hear the urgent shout,
But seventy thousand Zombies
Reply, "We're staying out!"

2. THE ZOMBIE PSALM

Mackenzie King is my shepherd,
I shall not wander,
He maketh me not to wear the G.S. Badge.
He leadeth me not across the still water,
He restoreth his vote,
He leadeth me along the path of Canada for his Party's sake.
Yea, though I move about from one camp to another,
I fear no draft,
For Mackenzie King is with me.
His Government and his Cabinet they comfort me.
He prepareth a table before me
In the presence of mine active enemies.
He does not clip my hair too short,
My glass runneth over with Canada's beer.
Surely the government will not alter its policy at this late date,
And I will dwell in the confines of Canada forever.

3. THE ZOMBIE PRAYER

We thank Thee, Lord, for Mackenzie King,
Who keeps his promise not to bring
Such divers trials and tribulations
As making us fight for Allied Nations,
Who looks Canadians in the eye
And says, "My Zombies shall not die."

We also thank, Thee, too, O Lord,
That he provides us with our board,
He gives us lodgings, clothes and guns,
But keeps us clear of nasty Huns.

And when our country fights the Japs,
And men are needed to fill the gaps,
We pray, dear Lord, he'll spare us boys,
And send those awful G.S. guys.

From active service, us preserve,
We really haven't got the nerve.
Content are we to serve him well
Who keeps us from the front-line hell,
Grant this, O Lord, and we will be
Always grateful unto Thee.
                                        Amen.

LETTER HOME

UNKNOWN

Thanks for the socks,
Oh, what a fit!
I used one for a hat
And the other for a mitt.

THE MULTIPEDES ON THE ROADS

E. J. PRATT

(Excerpt from Dunkirk*)*

Born on the blueprints,
They are fed by fire.
They grow their skin from carburized steel.
They are put together by cranes.
Their hearts are engines that do not know fatigue
In the perfection of their valves,
In the might of their systolic thrusts.
Their blood is petrol: Oil bathes their joints.
Their nerves are wire.
From the assembly lines they are put on inspection.
They pass tests,
Are pronounced fit by the drill-sergeants.
They go on parade and are the pride of the High Command.
They take, understand and obey orders.
They climb hills, straddle craters and the barbed barricades.
They defy bullets and shells.
Faster than Genghis' cavalry they speed,
Crueller than the hordes of Tamburlaine,
Yet unknowing and uncaring.
It is these that the rearguards are facing —
Creatures of conveyer belts,
Of precision tools and schedules.
They breathe through carburetted lungs;
If pierced, they do not feel the cut,
And if they die, they do not suffer death.
And Dunkirk stands between the rearguards and the sea.

WEDNESDAY, MAY 29

ROBERT FINCH

Early this morning, along the eastern pass,
A pale ship sails toward a tapestry
Of bellying darkness ripped with crimson claws,
Toward grimy beaches black with blocks of men
Gaunt in the chill, silently waiting their turn
To be taken off. In weaving smoke and flame
Of bomb, machine-gun, shell, rifle, they wait.
Those less near the redemptive hour are busy
Redeeming even this day in work and pleasure:
Water, food, ammunition, landed, carried
Up, the sick and injured carried down,
Meals cooked and eaten, footballs bunted round,
Trick-riding turns on army bicycles,
Paddling, and always always always the singing,
Somebody, one or many, incessantly singing,
While onto the studded beach more troops come flooding,
Belgians, the First French Army, other British,
And ever new blocks of men in the flaring darkness
Form up in silence and motionless wait the order
To join the blocks that move to embarkation
Through shifting smoke, down the long wooden gangway
Of the East Pier, two thousand men an hour,
Under a sluice of bombs that cripple ships,
Set them on fire and sink them, chaos of wreckage
That swift decision saves from clogging the harbour
While swift incision succours and saves the wounded
In sick-bays racked by fickle wind and surf.
Nearer the enemy draws on both sides, captures
Mardyck Fort to the west, Nieuport to the east,
Launches streamers of tanks, streamers of lorries,
Now, through Belgian surrender, avidly bounding
To the coast, garish with blaze for thirty miles,
Where, etched for thirty miles against the glare,
A belt of ships is looping troops away
Over the maps of oil that mark the graves

Of former ships; three destroyers go down,
Five troop-ships, eight other vessels, eleven disabled.
In spite of the wind, the surf, the gunning, the bombing,
To-day, thirty-eight thousand men are lifted.
The glass is rising, reports say calm to-morrow.

JUBILEE

PETER TAYLOR

August 19, 1942

Europe was discovering new orbits of pain,
worlds colliding, the iron roller pressing
cities into scrap, history dissolved, the insect armies
pulled shapeless from the beaches. Then Dieppe.

At dawn they cut fresh surf to reach the shingle
struggling piecemeal through the firesweep
to clear the town, until, by ebb-tide
retreat had turned into a grim collection.

What is this bloody touchstone to a nation?
Whispers in homes, files, typewriters
clicking inevitable volumes while masons
cut old stones to mark this ignorance and gift.

DIEPPE

GEORGE WHALLEY

Ebbed now the cold fear
that turns the will to water,
fear of waiting ebbed,
and fierce joy of assault,
and killing; the fine defiance,

the shout on the lips, the zip-
whine of bullets and shells;
the leading, the delight
of high endeavour certain
of quick victory.
Nothing was clear then
but sharp feelings of fear
and joy; and they are seared
so deeply into the soul
that any could see them, even
now that they have ebbed.

The dull smack, dull
thud, dull dark
dropping down under wounds.
And now he sits in a cobbled
square above the seawall;
head in hands, alone,
shaken, cold, utterly
desolate: the ships
gone, the friends ebbed
homeward. Was it ever
fun to be young, to attack
(face blackened), to lead,
to kill? All ebbed out
to the cold trembling dread
of a small boy climbing
a dark stair.

            The tide,
turned from ebb, is flooding,
washing about the tracks
and turrets of the tanks
that never cleared the shingle:
burned out, broken, awry;
startled, questioning yet,
as somehow the living no longer
have power or desire to question.

THIS WAS MY BROTHER

MONA GOULD

This was my brother
At Dieppe,
Quietly a hero
Who gave his life
Like a gift,
Withholding nothing.

His youth . . . his love . . .
His enjoyment of being alive . . .
His future, like a book
With half the pages still uncut —

This was my brother
At Dieppe —
The one who built me a doll house
When I was seven,
Complete to the last small picture frame,
Nothing forgotten.

He was awfully good at fixing things,
At stepping into the breach when he was needed.

That's what he did at Dieppe;
He was needed.
And even death must have been a little shamed
At his eagerness.

Mona Gould, the author, added the following note: "The poem is for 'Mook' (Lt.-Col. Howard McTavish, Royal Canadian Engineers, killed in action, Dieppe, 1942.)"

HONG KONG, 1941

RAYMOND SOUSTER

"You bastards are going with me
right to the top and we'll kill
every one of those bloody Japs,"
Sergeant-Major John Robert Osborn
told his sixty-five men.

(All that was left of "B" Company,
Winnipeg Grenadiers, a regiment
"not recommended for operational training,"
on December 19, 1941.)

And thirty minutes later
with now only thirty men left,
he stormed to the very top
of Mount Butler, then stayed there
for eight and a half long hours.

(Osborn, able-seaman at Jutland,
farmer in Saskatchewan,
Manitoba railway worker —
now at forty-two
a soldier at Hong Kong.)

"Dig, you sons-of-bitches,
dig like you've never dug before,
they'll be back for us very soon,"
he told them with a grin.

(Meanwhile, three thousand miles away,
in Ottawa, Mr. Ralston,
Canadian Minister of Defence:
"The garrison's position is undoubtedly,
for the time being anyway,
a very trying and difficult one.")

John Osborn, Regimental Sergeant-Major,
his bayonet caked thick with blood,
an ugly gash showing on his forearm,
would have damn well agreed with him. . . .)

And before long the Japs came back,
slinging grenades by the dozen,
and soon there were twelve,
then only six Grenadiers;
five finally as Osborn
threw himself on a grenade
he couldn't reach in time. . . .

Is there still a Mount Butler
in Hong Kong today?
If there is it should be called
John Osborn's Hill.

SICILIAN VIGNETTE

GEORGE WHALLEY

These guns could have worked
disaster in our assault.
So the blood of sleepy Italians
is splashed on a whitewashed wall.

Their boots are under their beds.
Their helmets hang by the door.
And the careful letters from home
are scattered on the floor.

154

YOU'LL GET USED TO IT

You'll get used to it.
You'll get used to it.
The first year is the worst year,
Then you get used to it.
You can scream and you can shout;
They will never let you out.
It serves you right, you so-and-so;
Why aren't you a naturalized Eskimo?

Just tell yourself it's marvellous.
You get to like it more and more and more.
You've got to get used to it!
And when you're used to it,
You'll feel just as lousy as you did before.

You'll get used to it!
You'll get used to it!
The first year is the worst year,
Then you get used to it.
You will never see your wife
For they've got you in for life.
It makes no difference who you are,
A soda jerk or movie star.

Freddy Grant composed the smash hit "You'll Get Used to It." He performed
this version, the earliest, in 1940 at Camp Q, near Monteith, northern
Ontario, where he was an alien internee.

Three Verses from the Italian Front

1. GUEST ARTIST

J. DAWSON

They brought Lily Pons and they brought Jascha Heifitz,
There was Irving Berlin and la belle Marlene Dietrich.
Bob Hope and Jack Haley came out here, I know,
With the purpose in mind of our own Army Show.
I saw the Tin Hats and the Forage Caps also;
I've heard singers (base) and chanteuses (contralto).
To morale-lifting agents I say simply, "Brother,
If you want real results — just you bring out my Mother!"

2. Q.M. OVERSIGHT

THOMAS GEOFFERY HANSON III

A signalman out "on the loose,"
Met a WAAF who said, "Why you goose,
    Your battledress pants
    Remind me of France —
They're so much Toulon and Toulouse."

3. SLIT TRENCH SOLILOQUY

E. J. CAUGHTY

When I am in the front line
And shells go whistling by,
I've often said it to myself
I'd sooner live than die.

MEDITATION AFTER AN ENGAGEMENT

DOUGLAS LePAN

Lack-lustre now the landscape, too long acquainted
With death and wounds. Only the orchard where
Persimmons smoulder in the darkening air,
Like cressets guttering to an orange glow,
Preserves the landscape the old masters painted;
A glimmer in green leaves and glossy bark,
A radiance rescued from the pouring dark,
A fragment of the glister of Uccello.

Through that green secrecy my limbs would drown
Drifting enfranchised down a still bay, preened
By art, a peacock lustre damascened
With meandering dreams and pleasures, where
        unconstrued
Would waters hide me with their amaranth crown.
Even the fishermen who fish night-long
With flares would never net my rapturous song,
Leafy with marvels like a romantic wood.

Pleasure? A romantic wood? The other trees
Have left the venom of a senseless flail
And on the threshing-floor are dying, pale
As wounded men on whom the darkness hardens.
The farm is pock-marked with a strange disease.
The craters suppurate an acid sea
That, spreading, blots out old calligraphy.
A peasant points and says, "These all were gardens."

No. I cannot from a few leaves twist
A sheltering chaplet even of despair,
When trees and fields for miles around are bare.

If there is any comfort, then I must find
It in the open where the dead insist
How cold the earth has turned. This lingering swoon
Of colour is ambushed fatally, and soon
The fruit will fall like kings in a rebel wind.

O entropy that has involved our hearts!
A mother kindles withered twigs beneath
A pot and lets them die for lack of breath.
The farmer risks the dull, gun-metalled sky
And, slouching bare-foot through the shell holes, starts
To shave more fodder from the dripping straw-stack,
Forgets his purpose and comes empty-handed back.
The age is guttering to senility.

But she (the woman who is my wisdom) writes
That every age has been faint-hearted, redeemed
By daring horsemen, whose gold stirrups gleamed
On the flanks of the lathered time, past the dark croup
Spattering brightness; and their extreme delights —
Turmoil, difficulty and a distant quarry —
Were frescoed as the background of their glory.
And I believe her — but hear no huntsmen up.

The soldiers, huddled in the night's neglect,
Know only that the weather here has broken,
Deep in their bones the coming snow has spoken
Death. With lonely men in the moon's eye
I stare at ruts and puddles that reflect
Clay-tarnished splendour and, in the doom of words,
Nail to my shuttered heart with pitted swords
The weather, exile and man's agony.

NORMANDY 1944

GEORGE WHALLEY

Forget about what's on the beaches. Tide,
wind and the blind muffling drift of sand
will care for that. Deeper inland, here
where the apples taste only the rumours of gales,
the wounds are subtler. One obliterating
sweep of a bulldozer crushes for all time
a sunken lane which never knew harsher uses
than murmur of lovers in mothlight. What do we care
for the splintered stillness of a Norman tower,
soiled (had it not been destroyed) by iron-shod
boots and spotter's glasses and the predatory
snap of a sniper's rifle? What to us
is the gnarled and immemorial apple orchard
under whose trees we heap up ammunition,
dig fox-holes and write V-letters home?
The tanks have made destructive harvesting
of fields patiently waiting for the scythe.
The bearded pale gold wheat and the poppies know
the sudden limp impersonality
of violent death. In Bayeux, while the guns
thunder round Caen preparing the final assault,
the houses, as though bemused, stare with blind
eyes at the tanks clattering over the cobbles
and the crowning impertinent insult of the jeeps.
And there's no wandering with a market basket,
no passing the time with gossip at a corner.
The silent villagers' eyes are dull, bewildered
with wondering how the refugees are faring.

Whether we do it or the enemy,
this second death in no wise rights the first.
Perhaps we need this blindness, need this hangman's
smiling complacency, because we know
the Army of Liberation strips the country girl
and, laughing, sets her to walk her native streets
naked and humbled in the lewd eye of the world.

ONE OF THE REGIMENT

DOUGLAS LePAN

In this air
Breathed once by artist and *condottier*,
Where every gesture of proud men was nourished,
Where the sun described heroic virtue and flourished
Round it trumpet-like, where the face of nature
Was chiselled by bright centuries hard as sculpture;
His face on this clear air and arrogant scene,
Decisive and impenetrable, is Florentine.

Where every hill
Is castled, he stands like a brooding tower; his will
An angry shadow on this cloudless sky,
Gold with the dust of many a panoply
And blazonings burnt up like glittering leaves;
His only cognizance his red-patched sleeves;
Fair hair his helmet; his glancing eye, the swagger
Of his stride are gallant's sword and dagger.

And in his mind
The sifting, timeless sunlight would not find
Memories of stylish Florence or sacked Rome,
Rather the boyhood that he left at home;
Skating at Scarborough, summers at the Island,
These are the dreams that float beyond his hand,
Green, but estranged across a moat of flame;
And now all bridges blown the way he came.

No past, no future
That he can imagine. The fiery fracture
Has snapped that armour off and left his bare
Inflexible, dark frown to pluck and stare
For some suspected rumour that the brightness sheds
Above the fruit-trees and the peasants' heads
In this serene, consuming lustrousness
Where trumpet-tongues have died, and all success.

Do not enquire
What he has seen engrained in stillest fire
Or what he purposes. It will be well.
We who have shared his exile can trumpet-tell
That underneath his wild and frowning style
Such eagerness has burned as could not smile
From coats of lilies or emblazoned roses.
No greater excellence the sun encloses.

THE ROAD TO NIJMEGEN

EARLE BIRNEY

December my dear on the road to Nijmegen
between the stones and the bitten sky
was your face

Not yours at first
but only the countenance of lank canals
and gathered stares
(too rapt to note my passing)
of graves with frosted billy-tins for epitaphs
bones of tanks beside the stoven bridges
and old men in the mist
hacking the last chips
from a boulevard of stumps

These for miles and the fangs of homes
where women wheeled in the wind
on the tireless rims of their cycles
like tattered sailboats,
tossing over the cobbles

and the children
groping in gravel for knobs of coal
or clustered like wintered flies
at the back of messhuts
their legs standing like dead stems out of their clogs

Numbed on the long road to mangled Nijmegen
I thought that only the living of others assures us
the gentle and true we remember as trees walking
Their arms reach down from the light of kindness
into this Lazarus tomb

So peering through sleet as we neared Nijmegen
I glimpsed the rainbow arch of your eyes
Over the clank of the jeep
your quick grave laughter
outrising at last the rockets
brought me what spells I repeat
as I travel this road
that arrives at no future
and what creed I can bring
to our daily crimes
to this guilt
in the griefs of the old
and the graves of the young

NIJMEGEN, HOLLAND, 1944

RAYMOND SOUSTER

"The Canadian Indians are coming,"
the German troops warned us solemnly,
that afternoon they left our city
for the very last time.

"You'll know them by their faces
painted red, blue and yellow,
from the way they loot your houses,
steal your food, rape your women.
So keep your blinds well down,
don't show fire-smoke,
hide your daughters in the attic,
and perhaps do some extra praying."

That's what the Germans told us,
so we trembled all night in our beds,
not wanting to wake in the morning.

Then peeked out through our front windows
very early to see slowly working their way
first down one street and then another,
the white, nervous faces of young boys
trying almost too hard to act
like tough, devil-may-care fighting men,
and just barely missing in the part.

I wept openly with joy
looking at each uncomplicated face,
knowing Holland was free at last,
knowing Holland was both safe and free.

EX-SERGEANT WHALEN TELLS THIS STORY

ALDEN NOWLAN

The Burgermeister,
                    that's what the Dutch
call their Mayors,
                    Burgermeisters,
the Burgermeister of Nijmegen,
he gave us a big spiel.
                    In English.
I still know some of it
        by heart,
although this was thirty years ago.

The Germans came
                    we got fed up with them.

The British came
              and showed us what to do.
The Americans came
              and told us how great they were.

Then the Canadians came

and so long as they had
    a bottle on the hip
        and a girl on the arm
they didn't give a damn
           who
ran the country.

Well!
naturally we gave
         the Burgermeister
three
cheers
and a tiger.
        But the joke of it was
the Brits and Yanks —
they thought he'd paid
them
    a compliment!

Poor silly buggers,
they cheered too.

NAVY

ROLL ALONG, WAVY NAVY

Roll along, Wavy Navy, roll along,
Roll along, Wavy Navy, roll along.
If they ask us who we are,
We're the RCNVR —
Roll along, Wavy Navy, roll along.

First of seven verses of the song sung by members of the Royal Canadian Naval
Volunteer Reserve who wore wavy stripes on their uniforms.

THE NAVAL CONTROL SERVICE
OFFICER ADDRESSES THE MASTERS

E. J. PRATT

(*Excerpt from* Behind the Log)

Good morning, gentlemen. It is a pleasure
To see familiar faces here today.
To such of you who have commanded ships
In earlier convoys what I have to say
Will be just dishing up the old instructions.
But since to many it is the first adventure,
I know you'll pardon me if I should cover
With some precision the important points.
Let me begin by saying that your convoy
Has, in its Commodore, one of the most
Renowned men in the Service. It is not
For me to talk at length about his fine
And honourable record. It is known
To all of you. He has of his free choice
Issued from his well-earned retirement
To place at the disposal of the Allies
His knowledge, skill, and practical seamanship.
Here at this table, gentlemen: Rear-Admiral
Sir Francis Horatio Trelawney-Camperdown!

GUNBOAT SORTIE

GEORGE WHALLEY

A few nights after Christmas we made the cold
crossing against a rapidly freshening wind.
Before the full dark came, Jupiter,
Sirius and Betelgeux appeared,
then Saturn below the delicate Pleiades.
The salt inflamed our eyes. The wind plucking
peremptorily at the eyelids stunned us.
The waves were brutal ponderances crushing
with slow energy against the boat.

As the moon rose quenching the sharp stars
we picked our way through the rocks that rise in
    abrupt
dark pinnacles out of deep water.
No light to guide, no monitory bell;
but the waves whitened each lurking rock to a pale
menace of foam. Suddenly we sighted
the black tower of Triagoz against
the luminous sky, and the low looming shadow
of France. Midnight. We stole up the hostile bay
until we could see the village, a homely cluster
of darkened cottages comfortably sleeping
around a slender spire on a dark hillside.

Through the surging rush and snap of the seas
there comes to us from the shore a single birdcry,
desolate and wild as a loon calling
the rain across a mirror-lake in the dusk.
Sensed but not seen, tormented but unchecked
by tumble of seas, the ground swell rolls
singly under, lifting the boat; mute
manifestos of the primal fact
until the shoal water trips it, ripping
the rind of its monstrous inscrutability,
curls its crest in a smooth sinuous burst

rippling into thunder. The moon in the surf
looks like the beam of a searchlight sweeping the coast.

Two hours pass. Our sense of danger is sharp
and clear as the village spire against the sky.
Then the job is done and we shape course for home,
with a full gale on the quarter and a full moon
setting us uplight to the enemy.
Into us flows an exhilarating peace
born of the wind and moonlight, and the grey
valleys between the phosphorescent crests,
and the thought of England ahead below the stars.
The cold misery of the coming and our fear
are purged and forgotten in our reverie.

Pirate shouts, "Look at them. Six of the bastards,
fine to port." We alter course towards them.
"Here it comes." And red and green and yellow
tracers crawl towards us lazily
looking like lights on a children's Christmas tree.

MEMO FROM A FREIGHTER

DICK DIESPECKER

U Boat, U Boat, stalking me,
You are the flower that opens in the night,
The white sweet sickly bloom of death;
You are the formless face that follows me
Into the trackless depths of sleep,
Swaying soundless with the rolling waves,
Whispering destruction with your lipless mouth;
You are the eyeless watcher in the deadly sea,
Hunting me through the darkness to the dawn,
Searching with electric fingers for my throat,
Waiting to hurl destruction through my steel walls,
To stab me with enormous blows,
Flinging me helpless to the boiling depths,
Pressing me down into the cold green breathless dark,

Leaving me there, a mangled hulk,
With only the waves to mark my resting place.
But if you find me so before the dawn,
And sink me with your deadly shafts,
There will be ten more such as I
To take my place; and you will wither before the sunset comes,
Torn by the slim steel terriers of the sea,
Plunging in tattered hideous death
To lie beside me on the ocean floor;
And none will weep above your sepulchre,
And there will be no more to take your place.

THE FIGHTING *P.R.*

GEORGE DANN

(To be sung to the tune, "The Strawberry Roan.")

Our city's Prince Rupert
Away in the West.
They gave us some presents,
They gave us the best,
A package of fags,
Wash-machine and guitar,
Was all that they sent
To the Fighting *P.R.*

Now our ship is manned
With twin four-inch guns.
We also have charges,
Some big heavy ones.
We are equipped with Asdics, Radar,
A real fightin' ship
Is the fighting *P.R.*

Now one night on convoy
We sighted a light.
We chased it all over
The ocean that night.

When morning dawned
'Twas only a star
That we had pursued
on the Fighting *P.R.*

I put in a request
To get me a draft.
Went up 'fore the Captain
But he only laughed.
He looked down at me,
And he said, "Har, har, har,
You're a permanent station
Aboard the *P.R.*"

Now if you want to get tight
But you can't find some chums
And you don't mind drinking
With a bunch of rum-dums,
Just hop in a cab,
Find the handiest bar,
And you'll find the crew
Off the Fighting *P.R.*

Now up on the Bridge,
When the guns go "glop,"
You should hear our old skipper
Just blowing his top.
Of all the old sea dogs
He beats them by far.
That's our old man
On the Fighting *P.R.*

Now we've finished our refit
And we're going quite soon.
So this is the end of my little tune.
We're going to sea
And we're going so far,
They'll never get me
Off this Fighting *P.R.*

George Dann ("Dan Dan the Radar Man") composed this ditty in 1944 when
he was senior radar operator aboard the corvette *Prince Rupert*.

SEA BURIAL

GEORGE WHALLEY

(*Excerpt from* Battle Pattern)

It is late afternoon.
The rainsquall has passed; but while it lasted
it brought down the visibility and stopped for a while
the bombing that made the survivors on the messdecks
pensive and inward-looking, smoking many cigarettes.
Fifteen minutes ago the Sub.,
a little pale from his interrupted work in the tiller flat,
reported to the bridge. So now would be a good time.

A Commander quietly leaves the bridge.
He was one with merry ways; but now his eyes
have a distant hungry lost silence in them.
You look at his borrowed grey trousers
and the monkey-jacket too big for him
and know why his eyes look the way they do.

The iron-deck abreast the torpedo tubes still glistens with rain;
and low cloud scurries smokily above the masthead.
A line of men ragged as the clouds,
girded in blankets, barefoot or shod with other men's boots,
pick their way aft. They are silent and their eyes are downcast.
Neither the white surge of water at the ship's side
nor the roar of exhaust fans
nor the blackened faces of the gunners at the multiple
touches them with wonder or comfort or irony.

And some there be which have no memorial,
who are perished as though they had never been.
We therefore commit their bodies to the deep,
where sorrow and pain are no more, neither sighing.

Concerning them that fall asleep:
They rest from their labours,
looking for the resurrection of the body.

Behold I tell you a mystery:
we shall not all sleep, but we shall all be changed
in a moment, in the twinkling of an eye.

Why do we also stand in jeopardy every hour?

Behold I tell you a mystery:
if there is no resurrection of the dead,
if the dead are not raised at all,
if in this life only we have hoped,
we are of all men most pitiable.

Why do we also stand in jeopardy every hour?

The men straggle forward,
picking their way against the motion of the ship.
The sky clears.
The alarm bells ring.
Aircraft approaching.
The sound is like a white-hot needle
plunged upward through the skull.

Blessed are the dead;
for since by man came death
why do we also stand in jeopardy?

SAIL ON

For all who sailed,
For all who prayed,
For those we mourn,
For those survived,
For blasted days,
For anguished nights,
For all brave men,
For freedom won,
May one sail on,
That none be lost.

These lines were composed by advertising
executive Jack Bush in 1983 for the
Canadian Naval Corvette Trust, the goal
of which is the restoration and preserva-
tion of the HMCS *Sackville*, the sole
remaining Canadian corvette from the
original Second World War fleet of 122.

AIR FORCE

HIGH FLIGHT

JOHN GILLESPIE MAGEE, JR.

Oh, I have slipped the surly bonds of earth,
And danced the skies on laughter-silvered wings;
Sunward I've climbed and joined the tumbling mirth
Of sun-split clouds — and done a hundred things
You have not dreamed of — wheeled and soared and swung
High in the sunlit silence. Hov'ring there,
I've chased the shouting wind along and flung
My eager craft through footless halls of air.
Up, up the long delirious, burning blue
I've topped the wind-swept heights with easy grace,
Where never lark, or even eagle, flew;
And, while with silent, lifting mind I've trod
The high untrespassed sanctity of space,
Put out my hand, and touched the face of God.

WATCHING AIRCRAFT
TAKE OFF FOR GERMANY

RAYMOND SOUSTER

For Carl Schaefer

Tonight these are the lucky ones
who watch from the tarmac
their comrades slowly, surely lifting off,

who'll later turn in sleep
hearing the engine-roar
of those even luckier ones
who've managed to come home again.

Then tomorrow night the ones
who've returned will watch these,
the watchers of tonight,
as they lift up, outbound.

And night after night
all that will ever change
will be the aircraft,
the faces watching them,

this war certainly will not change,
will have an even lustier
appetite for flesh.

WARTIME AIR BASE

AL PURDY

At 6.30 a.m. the siren screams
penetrating hospital and barracks
naked women like white dolls
fall out of dreams from windows
men drown into daylight
the guard changes at 8 o'clock
No crashes now for two weeks
and the dead men are not dead
Five miles up in overcast
the base is hardly visible
things wait between before and after
armies march and counter-march
but are seen to be standing still
in an old photograph
On the planet's surface blue uniforms
cross in front of the camera
then disappear forever
Airmen in coveralls flip an up-yours
salute at the C.O.'s car passing
Harvard trainers galumph the clouds

Fairey Battles whistle on the runway
cheerful as steam kettles
Hurricanes blast towed targets
they turn to confetti
Ten miles up you can't see the base
but there's nobody there to not-see
Nineteen days without a crash
the dying men are still alive
The chaplain talks about sin on Sunday
what he really talks about is life
Women in uniforms are not de-sexed
but camp followers who caught up
Berlin London Dresden and those places
are only dream towns
The parade ground bakes in noon sun
control tower voices stop
everybody half asleep
nobody a.w.o.l.
the dead men move slowly
toward what they think is choice
it is one of those moments
when a towel in somebody's bathroom
might fall unnoticed
or a leaf drift down
lacking any reason to stay on the tree
Ten miles up there is nothing
unless you can imagine a face
that pays no attention to you
it looks the other way

THE HEART TO CARRY ON

BERTRAM WARR

Every morning from this home
I go to the aerodrome.
And at evening I return
Save when work is to be done.

Then we share the separate night
Half a continent apart.

Many endure worse then we:
Division means by years and seas.
Home and lover are contained,
Even cursed within their breast.

Leaving you now, with this kiss
May your sleep tonight be blest,
Shielded from the heart's alarms
Until morning I return.
Pray tomorrow I may be
Close, my love, within these arms,
And not lie dead in Germany.

RAID ON THE RUHR, 1945

RAYMOND SOUSTER

For Art Servage

Bomb-selection switches on,
arming switch, bombsight switch okay,
repeater compass in good working order,
altimeter shipshape —

this, his last check made ahead of time,
left him a minute when he leaned back on his knees
in the bombardier's compartment and looked out ahead
through the moulded perspex nose
of "O" for "Oboe" at the darkness streaked
with yellow beams of searchlights, red, green-blue
of sky-markers, brown puffs of flak-fire,
and dead ahead the ghost-black silhouette
of a Hally banking hard into its bomb-run. . . .

Then he'd had his eyeful of hell: tried to forget
his heart beating faster, sweat underneath his armpits,

frozen feet, cold hands, their four engines' body-shaking roar,
tried to bring all his mind's focus back
to the head of his bombsight in front of him
swaying cobra-like to the aircraft's motion,
with him the snake-charmer very soon to be called
to do his little trick with the bombsight's hairlines,
dropping his twelve bulging canisters one per second
into the spreading crimson glow, sending his cargo
of incendiaries whistling down: stoking the fire-storms,
blackening the ruins, piling high the corpses
("We're going to shift the rubble around a little"
was the way the Briefing Officer had put it). . . .

He crouched now, eyes only on his pet snake,
counting the lifetime of minutes
to death or deliverance.

IN MEMORY OF JAMES EAGLESON, R.C.A.F.

DOUGLAS LOCHHEAD

I

In what glorious air
an acrobat he grew,
sailing circus boy
in his net of air,
confident,
setting the Mitchell always down
and running out for one
last bow. Roar
of engine and love a limit
he knew, he knew so much
the crew, no trapeze
was that high, they could not
swing laughing and tense

Berlin, Hamburg, Bremen,
a tangled run to Ruhr
and back to pile out like apes
swinging from harness into
the happy jungle of their own.
Face in a NAAFI mug
and letters from home.

II

Trip of hammer and hell
black eruption of sky
and shell in September sun
and a rattling chance to go in
low and come out
like swimmers.

In the eyes quickly closed,
in the captured light, there came
sudden heat of red and white
filling the cabins of their skulls
with its close warmth
dull and dry.

The left motor hit square.
And in that minute
of war and witness
they were headed down.

HYMN FOR THOSE IN THE AIR

DUNCAN CAMPBELL SCOTT

(To the Royal Canadian Air Force)

Eternal Father by Whose Might
    The firmament was planned,

Who set the stars their paths of light,
   Who made the sea and land,
Thou Who art far yet near,
   In the bright Now and Here,
And where the Void is sleeping,
   Take them who dare to fly
Into Thy keeping.

Guide them who move through dark and cloud
   Parting the pathless sky,
Sustain them when the storm is loud
   Till night and storm are by;
Driving through snow and sleet
   When wild the head-winds beat,
Thy sovereign Will commanding,
   Bring them who dare to fly
To a safe landing.

Lead them who, dauntless, mount the height
   Of the embattled air,
Through piercing shell, through searching light,
   Hold and be with them there;
Keep them in life or death
   Mindful of One Who saith,
Where the wild birds shall gather
   Not the least sparrow falls
Without the Father.

Lift up the souls who yet aspire
   To move within Thy Will,
Who rise above the World's desire,
   Foiled but unconquered still,
Triumphant in Thy Might,
   Gather them into Light,
The Valiant who have striven,
   Winged with Immortal Joy
Into Thy Heaven.

AFTERMATH

MAY 8TH, 1945

ROY DANIELLS

They tell me the war is over, at last are ended
Wounds and death, exile and suffering.
Spring is here and a bird sits chattering,
Hope will be stirred, hearts moved and grief suspended,
And life go on as was at first intended.
All day the Winnipeg wind has kept on blowing;
Now the blue sky hangs steady, snowing;
They say the minister's speech today was splendid.

The war is over — men will be back again
To harrow the plains, go prospecting for gold;
The nations will resume their ordered plan,
Building bright cities where rare goods are sold;
And truth and right their former place recover;
And prayers ascend to heaven. The war is over.

REMEMBERING ESQUIMALT

ROBIN SKELTON

For Frank Fryett, who, after several years in a Japanese Prisoner of War Camp near Nagasaki, was repatriated to a Rehabilitation Centre at Esquimalt on Vancouver Island

For rehabilitation
his camp was Esquimalt.
I remembered the kelp
in the tangling sea,
and the English gardens;

he remembered snow,
and eating meat, and
walking alone at night,

those years ago. V.J. Day
he'd seen a mirror.
"Christ," he said, "I'm
bent as a bloody crone!"
"You've had that crook back
all the bloody time
we've been in the mine!" they said;
he hadn't known.

And marching through Nagasaki,
"It looked like a flower
among the stones," he said,
"a cup and saucer
melted and hardened back
into folds of petals.
Lovely it was," he said,
"but I felt sick

thinking about it after."
We drank to Esquimalt,
all that clean blue air.
"One day," he said,
"on the ship from Java
we saw a tanker struck,
and the bastards burning and
running about like mad

ants, all burning whether
they jumped or not.
The sea was on fire," he said.
"We laughed and clapped
and cheered and stamped
to see the buggers trapped.
It isn't nice to think of
the way you get,

or even some things you've seen.
I liked Esquimalt.
They asked us to dances."
He picked up his stick.
"A bit like a rose," he said,
"I should have kept it.
That was one of the things
I should have kept."

DEDICATION

RALPH GUSTAFSON

"They shall not die in vain," we said.
"Let us impose, since we forget
The hopeless giant alphabet,
Great stones above the general dead,"
The living said.

"They shall not be outdone in stones.
Generously, sculptured grief shall stand
In general over numbered bones
With book and index near at hand
For particular sons.

"And we the living left in peace
Will set aside such legal date
At such and suchlike time or state
Or place as meet and fitting is,
Respecting this."

O boy, locked in the grisly hollow,
You who once idly peeled a willow-
switch, whistling, wondering at the stick
Of willow's whiteness clean and slick,
Do not believe that we shall bury
You with words: aptly carry

Cloth flowers, proxy for love.
O we have done with granite grief
And silk denials: summing you
Within the minutes' silence — two!
More than you had need to target
Hate, against the pitiless bullet's
Calculated greed oppose
Heart's anger: falling, gave to us
What power to lance the pocket of
An easy past, what use of love
Teaching children's laughter loud
On shutters in an evil street,
What edge, O death, of days, delight?
What linch of love, spate of sun?
And shall we with a sedentary noun
Signature receipt, having had read
The catechism of the generous dead?

You who live, see! These,
These were his hills where laughter was
And counted years of longing, grain
And wintry apples scorched in sun,
Of corded hemlock deep in snow.
Here at his seven birches growing
Oblique by the boulder the fence has stopped —
Rusted wire, posts lopped
For staking. To circle love, he said.
And there are other fables made:
Of plough and intricate loom; the broken
Soldier on the sill; and latin
Parchment framed, conferring letters
On hooded death; the axe the motto
Against the wall; abandoned hills.

Fables for stout reading. Tales
Listened to by twice-told death.
Our tongue how silent, muscles lithe
O land, hoist by the lag-end of little
Deeds? What lack of monstrous metal,

Monumental mouths; over
This land what love, wheel, lever
Of God, anchorage, pivot of days,
Remembering?

    Old and certain the sea,
The mountain-tilted sky, old,
Older than words, than you are old,
Boy, who never thought to point the hill
With dawn! Only as these, our telling:

As men labour: as harvest done:
At dusk a joyful walking home.
Of nearer things: how he was young,
And died, a silent writing down.

15

THE KOREAN WAR

The Korean War was a war between North and South Korea that involved world powers. It began on June 25, 1950, with the invasion of South Korea by North Korea. The Canadian Army Special Force, a volunteer brigade, fought as part of the United Nations Command under General Douglas MacArthur and his successor Lieutenant General Matthew B. Ridgeway. Canadians helped to free Seoul, the Kap'young Valley, and the Imjin River. The Chinese assault near Hill 187 was repulsed with Canadian losses. The armistice was signed at Panmunjom on July 27, 1953. Canada sent 21,940 soldiers to serve in Korea, and an additional 7,000 served from the cease-fire to the end of 1955. Five hundred and sixteen Canadians died in Korea in a war that was unpopular on the home front. The three selections from the *Princess Patricia's Canadian Light Infantry Regimental Song Book* are flanked by the ironic thoughts of George Johnston and the passionate final thoughts of Private Pat O'Connor. They are indeed his final thoughts. A stretcher-bearer with the Royal Canadian Regiment, O'Connor was killed in Chinese gunfire on May 30, 1951. This handwritten poem, his only known poetic work, was found among his personal effects. It expressed and continues to express the sentiments of servicemen and others who fought in Korea.

WAR ON THE PERIPHERY

GEORGE JOHNSTON

Around the battlements go by
Soldier men, against the sky —
Violent lovers, husbands, sons,
Guarding my peaceful life with guns.

My pleasures, how discreet they are:
A little booze, a little car,
Two little children and a wife
Living a small suburban life.

My little children eat my heart;
At seven o'clock we kiss and part,
At seven o'clock we meet again;
They eat my heart and grow to men.

I watch their tenderness with fear
While on the battlements I hear
The violent, obedient ones,
Guarding my family with guns.

THE RIC-A-DAM DOO

The Princess Pat's Battalion
They sailed across the Herring Pond,
They sailed across the Channel too,
And landed there with the Ric-A-Dam-Doo,
                    Dam-Doo, Dam-Doo.

The Princess Pat's Battalion Scouts
They never knew their whereabouts,
If there's a pub within a mile or two,
You'll find them there with the Ric-A-Dam-Doo,
                    Dam-Doo, Dam-Doo.

The Lewis Guns are always true
To every call of the Ric-A-Dam-Doo.
They're always there with a burst or two
Whenever they see the Ric-A-Dam-Doo,
                    Dam-Doo, Dam-Doo.

The Bombers of the Princess Pat's
Are scared of naught, excepting rats,
They're full of pep and dynamite too,
They'd never lose the Ric-A-Dam-Doo,
                    Dam-Doo, Dam-Doo.

The Transport of the Princess Pat's
Are all dressed up in Stetson hats.
They shine their brass and limbers too
I believe they'd shine the Ric-A-Dam-Doo,
                    Dam-Doo, Dam-Doo.

Old Number Three, our company
We must fall in ten times a day
If we fell out 'twould never do
For then we'd lose the Ric-A-Dam-Doo,
                    Dam-Doo, Dam-Doo.

Old Charlie S., our Major dear,
Who always buys us rum and beer,
If there's a trench in a mile or two
You'll find him there with the Ric-A-Dam-Doo,
                    Dam-Doo, Dam-Doo.

Old Ackity-Ack, our Colonel grand,
The leader of this noble band,
He'd go to Hell and charge right through
Before he'd lose the Ric-A-Dam-Doo,
                    Dam-Doo, Dam-Doo.

Old Hammy Gault, our first PP,
He led this band across the sea,
He'd lose an arm, or leg or two
Before he'd lose the Ric-A-Dam-Doo,
     Dam-Doo, Dam-Doo.

And then we came to Sicily
We leapt ashore with vim and glee
The Colonel said the Wops are through
Let's chase the Hun with the Ric-A-Dam-Doo,
     Dam-Doo, Dam-Doo.

In '48 the Princess Pat's,
Went out to earn their wings and hats,
They jumped from planes and gliders too,
To show their pride in the Ric-A-Dam-Doo,
     Dam-Doo, Dam-Doo.

Stand up! Hook up! Stand in the door
The Pat's are first as they were before,
Across the seas or through the blue
You'll find in front the Ric-A-Dam-Doo,
     Dam-Doo, Dam-Doo.

The Ric-A-Dam-Doo, pray what is that?
'Twas made at home by Princess Pat,
It's Red and Gold and Royal Blue,
That's what we call the Ric-A-Dam-Doo,
     Dam-Doo, Dam-Doo.

Regimental song of the Princess Patricia's Canadian Light Infantry

KOREAN SAKI

UNKNOWN

(Tune: "Cigarettes & Whisky & Wild Wild Women")

I enlisted last August to come to this place,
With a resolute heart and a smile on my face,
But now that I've been here six months I'll tell you
Of Pom Pom and Saki and what it'll do.

CHORUS

Don't touch that Godam Korean Saki
It'll drive you crazy, it'll drive you insane.
Don't touch that Godam Korean Saki
It'll drive you crazy, it'll drive you insane.
I once was a clean cut Canadian lad,
My morals weren't good but they really weren't bad,
Now the lines on my face make a well-written page
My hair's falling out and I look twice my age.

It all started back at a place called Miryang,
We were Cee Bee'd but I went with the gang,
We jumped camp and went to a house of ill fame,
Where the women all drank and we learned a new game.

CHORUS

Those nights on the hill they were colder than ice,
So when canned heat they gave us, we thought it was nice,
We squeezed it and boiled it and drank it with glee,
Much worse by far than Korean Saki.

CHORUS

There on the cross at the head of my grave,
From Pom Pom and Saki, here lies a poor slave,
Take warning O Soldier, take warning young man,
Stay away from Korea as long as you can.

CHORUS

GHOST JUMPERS IN THE SKY

UNKNOWN

(To the tune of "Ghost Riders in the Sky")

An old jumper went walking out one dark and stormy night,
He heard some motors roaring and he knew it was a kite,
He heard some jumpers singing as they flew on thru the night,
They knew their fate was coming, but they sang with all their
    might,

"Geronimo!" Look out below!
The Ghost Jumpers in the Sky.

The dispatcher lay there looking out for the Drop Zone coming
    up,
The jumpers leaped out of their seats like cats and started
    hooking up,
And as they closed up to the door, you could hear their mournful
    whine,

"Geronimo!" Look out below!
The Ghost Jumpers in the Sky.

Their eyes were dim, their faces gaunt,
Their smocks were soaked with sweat,
They hated jumping worse than you but they're still jumping yet.
So Jumper change your ways today, and believe this story true,
For you'll never know when you will join those Jumpers in the
    Blue.

"Geronimo!" Look out below!
The Ghost Jumpers in the Sky.

And as he stood there tensely looking up, he heard one call his
    name,
"If you would join our hellish world then you just jump again."
A bolt of fear went through him as he heard them scream in pain.
He knew that he was going to fail
And he'd never jump again.

"Geronimo!" Look out below!
The Ghost Jumpers in the Sky.
The Ghost Jumpers in the Sky.

KOREA

PRIVATE PAT O'CONNOR

There is blood on the hills of Korea
'Tis blood of the brave and the true
Where the 25th Brigade battled together
Under the banner of the Red White and Blue
As they marched over the fields of Korea
To the hills where the enemy lay
They remembered the Brigadier's order:
These hills must be taken today
Forward they marched into battle
With faces unsmiling and stern
They knew as they charged the hillside
There were some who would never return
Some thought of their wives and mothers
Some thought of their sweethearts so fair
And some as they plodded and stumbled
Were reverentially whispering a prayer
There is blood on the hills of Korea
It's the gift of the freedom they love
May their names live in glory forever
And their souls rest in heaven above.

16

PEACEKEEPING AND PROTEST

"Peacekeeping and Protest" remains the title of this section, despite the absence from its pages of songs, poems, or verses composed by or about Canadian peacekeepers at home or abroad. The reason for this absence is simple enough. The present editors could find no such compositions. Yet they experienced little difficulty in locating compositions devoted to protest, for there was found to be no shortage of songs, poems, or verses composed during the years that peacekeeping became a hallmark of Canada's foreign policy. Perhaps the absence and the presence are related. Maybe peacekeepers are protesters, and protesters peacekeepers.

Canada's earliest peacekeeping operations helped bring peace to Kashmir in 1949, Palestine in 1953, and Indochina in 1954. Operations linked with the United Nations may be dated from the Suez Crisis of 1956. Lester B. Pearson, president of the UN's General Assembly at the time of trouble in the Suez, was successful in separating the belligerents and in establishing a peace-monitoring force. For his effort he was awarded the Nobel Prize for Peace in 1957. In his acceptance speech, he noted the disparity between the provisions for peace and the preparations for war, saying, "The grim fact is that we prepare for war like precocious giants and for peace like retarded pygmies."

The UN Emergency Force came about largely through Pearson's actions, and Canada supplied the earliest volunteers. Indeed, over the years, Canadian officers and men have taken part in more UN peacekeeping operations than officers and men of any other country. Canadians have served in a dozen or more foreign countries, and Canadian troops are currently performing peacekeeping functions in Korea, Cyprus, and the Golan Heights area on the Syria-Israel border.

Keeping the peace may be a moral undertaking, but it is not the most uplifting, at least for the stay-at-homes. Canadians have turned into harsh critics of the actions of other countries, notably the superpowers. Canada remained aloof from the war in Vietnam (except for supplying peacekeepers in 1954–73) but did benefit from the manufacture of military equipment for use in Vietnam. It is important to note, however, that many Canadians legally crossed the border and enlisted in the U.S. forces; and if the exact number is not known, figures as high as forty thousand have been cited. It is known that 56 Canadians died fighting on Vietnam's soil. Canadians let the dictates of their consciences be known but remained safely within the orbits of NORAD and NATO. We agreed not to explode nuclear devices but allowed our airspace to be used as testing ranges for nuclear carrier systems. We agreed not to manufacture nuclear weapons but supplied the technology to little dictatorships.

In sum, this section is something of a stocktaking and a stockpile. It begins with a protest poem, "Lest We Forget," written by F. R. Scott in 1945, and draws attention to what is now called the military-industrial complex. It is followed by a protest verse published in 1955 by Joe Wallace, who was, curiously, a Canadian Roman Catholic Communist.

Buffy Sainte-Marie's "Universal Soldier" is an antiwar song from the peace and protest movements of the 1960s. Other songs composed and sung by this native performing artist that could be included are "Soldier Blue" and "My Country, 'Tis of Thy People You're Dying." If anthologies were endless, it would be possible to represent Stringband, as well as an earlier group called the Travellers, not to mention such compositions as Neil Young's "Ohio" (about the Kent State shootings) and Bruce Cockburn's "If I Had a Rocket Launcher" (with such lines as "Cry for Guatemala, with a corpse in every gate / If I had a rocket launcher I would not hesitate"). It is interesting to note that Country Joe MacDonald, the U.S. folk singer, has recorded an album of Robert W. Service's war verse.

The Canadian Armed Forces patrolled the streets of Montreal

and Ottawa at the height of the October Crisis of 1970. This war against terrorism gave Canadians their first taste of martial law since 1945. Al Purdy captures the quality of the experience in his longish poem on the crisis. The section closes with a distanced look at the war in Vietnam and a consideration of a Second World War memorial.

"This military story of Canada is a bold and mighty thing, and yet it is a bald tale and unadorned, a tale of those simple virtues of courage, endurance and self-sacrifice which war, for all its horrors and wanton destruction, seems to evoke in men inspired by a common sense of purpose. Perhaps out of this comradeship of arms, this memory of a heroic past, will some day come that sense of inward unity which is born of perils shared and victories won."

— George F. G. Stanley, *Canada's Soldiers: The Military History of an Unmilitary People*

LEST WE FORGET

F. R. SCOTT

The British troops at the Dardanelles
Were blown to bits by British shells
    Sold to the Turks by Vickers.
And many a brave Canadian youth
Will shed his blood on foreign shores,
And die for Democracy, Freedom, Truth,
With his body full of Canadian ores,
Canadian nickel, lead, and scrap,
Sold to the German, sold to the Jap,
    With Capital watching the tickers.

SUMMER WILL COME
WHEN WE WIN THE SPRING

JOE WALLACE

To fight for peace is at times a trouble
So is radio-active rubble.

I'd sooner take my girl to a show
Where it was once the weeds won't grow.

Logan to Lansdowne, Queen to St. Clair,
I looked for her. There was nothing there.

How would I feel should this occur?
To fight for peace is to fight for her.

No one is born or lives alone,
In guarding others we guard our own.

To fight for peace is a lovely thing
Summer will come when we win the Spring.

Birds will blossom and blossoms sing
Summer will come when we win the Spring.

UNIVERSAL SOLDIER

BUFFY SAINTE-MARIE

He's five foot two and he's six feet four,
    He fights with missiles and with spears.
He's all of thirty-one and he's only seventeen,
    He's been a soldier for a thousand years.

He's a Cath'lic, a Hindu, an atheist, a Jain,
    A Buddhist and a Baptist and a Jew.
And he knows he shouldn't kill and he knows he always
    Will kill you for me my friend and me for you.

And he's fighting for Canada, he's fighting for France,
    He's fighting for the U.S.A.
And he's fighting for the Russians and he's fighting for Japan
    And he thinks we'll put an end to war this way.

And he's fighting for democracy, he's fighting for the Reds,
    He says it's for the peace of all.
He's the one who must decide who's to live and who's to die
    And he never sees the writing on the wall.

But without him how would Hitler have condemned him at
        Dachau,
    Without him Caesar would've stood alone.
He's the one who gives his body as a weapon of the war.
    And without him all this killin' can't go on.

He's the universal soldier and he really is to blame.
His orders come from far away no more.
They come from here and there and you and me,
And, brothers, can't you see,
This is not the way we put an end to war.

THE PEACEABLE KINGDOM

AL PURDY

(In Ottawa, after the War Measures Act is invoked against the F.L.Q.)

Friday, Oct. 16: Along Elgin Street
traffic crawls at four o'clock
attachés with briefcases
of importance on Wellington
expensive mistresses and wives
of diplomats walking dogs
and babies in Rockcliffe Park
two Carleton students with lettered signs
VIVE le F.L.Q. on Parliament Hill
the Mounties don't lay a finger on them
below the Peace Tower
cabinet ministers interviewed on TV
inside the House
orators drone and wrangle as usual
in a way almost reassuring
In Quebec the Fifth Combat Group
from Valcartier occupies Montreal
paratroopers fly in from Edmonton
infantry from the Maritimes
And the P.M.'s comment
on bleeding hearts who dislike guns
"All I can say is go on and bleed
it's more important to keep law and order. . . ."
All this
in the Peaceable Kingdom

Saturday, October 17: No change
the two kidnapped men are still missing
In the House of Commons politicians
turn into statesmen very occasionally
Reilly on CTV news demands Trudeau resign
Eugene Forsey does not agree
Yesterday driving to Ottawa
with my wife
citizens of no Utopia
red autumn leaves on Highway #7
— thinking of the change come over us
and by us I mean the country
our character and conception of ourselves
thinking of beer-drinkers in taverns
with loud ineffectual voices disagreeing
over how to escape their own limitations
men who have lost their way in cities
onetime animals trapped inside tall buildings
farmers stopped still in a plowed furrow
that doesn't match the other straight lines
as a man's life turns right or left from the norm
No change in the news
N.D.P. and P.C. members condemn the government
Crèditiste Real Caouette does not
Diefenbaker thunders at the P.M.
a prophet grown old
Police raids continue in Montreal

Sunday, Oct. 18: Pierre Laporte found dead in a green Chev
outside St. Hubert shot in the head
hands tied behind his back murdered
A note from James Cross found in a church
asking police to call off the hunt for him
Crowds gather on Parliament Hill
for the same reason as myself
and stand close to the heart of things
perhaps if some were not before
they have become Canadians
as if it were not beneath them

gathered here to mourn for something
we did not know was valuable
the deathbed of innocence
mocked at by foreign writers
the willingness to pretend
our illusions were real
gone now
Soon we shall have refugees escaping the country
expatriates of the spirit and the body politic
and men in prison raving about justice
defectors beyond the reach
of what we had supposed was freedom
and the easy switchers of loyalty
will change ideas and coats and countries
as they do elsewhere and are no loss
Well
I suppose these things are easy to say
and some think sadness is quite enjoyable
I guess it is too
but this is not an easy sadness
like my own youth full of tears and laughter
in tough middle-age when I'm not
listening anymore sings to me sometimes
Beyond the death of Laporte
and the possible death of James Cross
the deathbed of something else
that is worth being mocked
by cynics and expatriate writers
— the quiet of falling leaves perhaps
autumn rains
long leagues of forest and the towns
tucked between hills for shelter
our own unguarded existence
we ransom day by day of our short lives

Driving west from Ottawa
we stop at a roadside park for lunch
beside a swift narrow black river
looped into calm by the park

thinking in this backwater
how the little eddy that is my life
and all our lives quickens
and bubbles break as we join
the mainstream of history
with detention camps and the smell of blood
and valid reasons for writing great novels
in the future the past closing around
and leaving us where I never wanted to be
in a different country from the one
where I grew up
where love seemed nearly an affectation
but not quite
beyond the Peaceable Kingdom

ON THE RENEWAL OF BOMBING IN VIETNAM, DECEMBER, 1972

ELI MANDEL

At the sight of this photograph
forming itself out of headlines and print
what should a poet do but cry out
that the dead are no less real
for falling into pictures of ruined cities

I do not mean to speak as a prophet
that cherished tone now detached
as if voice itself could be flung into space
without body
              At my kitchen table
The Toronto Star lies beside tall salt cellars
and where Bess Truman stares
with her closed gaze
                      Nadezhda Mandelstam's
Hope Against Hope, I notice, wears its purple
cover like a funeral robe

Tonight in our cities no doubt some
one will cry out
                    my daughter
sees in her dark room nameless horrors
and like photographs
                    silent and distant
the dead will fall
                    in the sum of
all days, nights, deaths, stars,
I hear this poem like a disembodied voice
less powerful than even a composition
made out of lead type and black ink

THE BRONZE PIPER

MILTON ACORN

Many Islanders fought World War II in the North Nova Scotia Highlanders.
There's this monument in New Glasgow, N.S.

In a park by the river in New Glasgow
stands a kilted piper playing a dirge;
with all round the plinth of the monument
(so many in so small a town)
the names of the dead in the First World War.

This was put up by the citizens
and of course most of the names are Scotch;
survivors Scotch too for they calculated
                    to a nicety in 1930
. . . how large a plinth for how many names.

Ten years after came another war
so behind they had to put up another stone
for names of the new born new dead; but
this time took precautions;
left a blank square yard and a half on the
                    back of the stone.

But . . . again but . . . when you look round the stone
you find this is not a monument
        but an advertisement.
    for the names of two entities
        living in law
that of a monument company
and a firm of architects
are there (though the sculptor's name is absent.

In a park by the river in New Glasgow
stands a kilted piper playing a dirge
all in bronze, though not kept shone
                            :   .
all in silence
            Still you know it's a dirge
for the dead, some of whom could be husky today
: and for . . .
            some of them hoped . . .
What exactly did they fight for?
        Yanks?
        to claim their victory?
        as if it was over themselves?
        their nation prisoner?
May the poem not end here;
                        the last note
not be a dirge . . .

17

FUTURE BATTLES

It is often said that Canadians have never engaged in a battle or a war of their own making, that Canada is one of the few countries that has never raided or invaded another land for national gain. Our country's soldiers remain "on guard" because they are, indeed, guards.

No one knows the future, so no one knows how long this tradition of trust and honour will continue. Nostradamuses are no help, especially with the threat of nuclear annihilation on the horizon. But one trusts that the moral momentum of the past will carry over into the future.

The final poem in this collection is Earle Birney's "World War III." Although it expresses current concerns, it is not a recent poem. Birney wrote it at Hood Point, Bowen Island, British Columbia, in 1947. It brings to life the poet's continuing and mounting concern for the continuity of life — and the need to change ourselves before we try to change the world.

WORLD WAR III

EARLE BIRNEY

Will it be much as before?
Shall we learn to wear like fraternity pins
the deaths of our friends once more?
Will it be hard to keep track of the Finns
and who should be shot in the Balkans?
Of course we shall all play the rôle of the chicks
but who will be hooded like falcons?

Should youth as usual take the hint
politely declining to argue with print
permitted once more to gouge and smother
and mailed the weekly blessing from mother?
Will some save their money and some their lives
acquire new skills or noses or wives?

Shall we both fight superbly and sometimes with wrath
bemedal the brave and the bold psychopath,
the captains of industry, colonels or better,
the widow, the girl in the tightest sweater?

Will it be much as went by
with a leave between each slaughtering session
for movies where only the enemy die
and no time left to recall a depression?
When pulses and birth rates leap
when plagues are confined to the backward nations
and poets can ride in a jeep?

Or will it be more than before?
Will even Americans eat much less
restrict their water as well as their press
and bleed in the corner store?
Will all of the old be killed
including the guilty, will space be filled
with blood like a Sunday paper?

Shall we all be scientists then and find
a method with plasma and plastic mind
to keep nearly everyone half-alive?
Shall we save humanely in leaden hive
our cretins, Creons, movable art,
and declared insane, for another start?

May we even dispense with the opening dream
of oldfashioned wars when we fancied the gleam
of a world sunrise, in the flash of the Sten
and peace was only postponed again?

Or will it be something quite new?
Before the pale clouds have cast their seed
before the twoheaded children succeed
can the brain teach the heart what to do?
Can love bend the earth to his will
can we kill only that which drives us to kill
and drown our deaths in a Creed?

SOURCES

PREFACE
"O Canada." 29 Elizabeth, c. 5. *The Canada Gazette*, Part III, 30 June 1980.

1. INDIAN BATTLES
"Iroquois War Song." Anna Brownell Jameson. *Winter Studies and Summer Rambles in Canada*. 1838.
"At the Long Sault." Archibald Lampman. *At the Long Sault and Other Poems*. 1943. Edited by E. K. Brown.
"Madeleine Verchères." William Henry Drummond. *Dr. Drummond's Complete Poems*. 1926.
"Watkwenies." Duncan Campbell Scott. *Selected Poems of Duncan Campbell Scott*. 1931.

2. THE ENGLISH AND THE FRENCH
"The Captured Flag." Arthur Weir. *Songs of the Great Dominion*. 1889. Edited by W. D. Lighthall.
"Amis chantons la gloire." *The French Tradition in America*. Columbus, S.C.: University of South Carolina Press, 1969. Edited by Yves F. Zoltvany.
"General Wolfe." *Singing Our History*. Toronto: Doubleday, 1984. Edited by Edith Fowke.
"Dead March for Sergeant MacLeod." Al Purdy. *Sex and Death*. Toronto: McClelland and Stewart, 1973. Used by permission of McClelland and Stewart Limited, Toronto.

3. THE AMERICAN INVASION
"Marching Down to Old Quebec." *Singing Our History*. Toronto: Doubleday, 1984. Edited by Edith Fowke.
"Spirit of 1775–1975." Raymond Souster. *Extra Innings*. Ottawa: Oberon Press, 1977. Reprinted from *Collected Poems of Raymond Souster* by permission of Oberon Press.

4. THE WAR OF 1812
"Come All You Bold Canadians." *Singing Our History*. Toronto: Doubleday, 1984. Edited by Edith Fowke.
"The Battle of Queenston Heights." *Singing Our History*. Toronto: Doubleday, 1984. Edited by Edith Fowke.
"The Ballad of Queenston Heights." Francis Sparshott. *The Naming of the Beasts*. Windsor: Black Moss Press, 1979. Reprinted by permission of the author.
"Tecumseh's Death." Major John Richardson. *Songs of the Great Dominion*. 1889. Edited by W. D. Lighthall.
"The *Chesapeake* and the *Shannon*." *Singing Our History*. Toronto: Doubleday, 1984. Edited by Edith Fowke.
"Brock." Charles Sangster. *The Hesperus and Other Poems and Lyrics*. 1860.
"Laura Secord." Raymond Souster. *Ten Elephants on Yonge Street*. 1965. Reprinted from *Collected Poems of Raymond Souster* by permission of Oberon Press, Ottawa.

5. THE MASSACRE OF SEVEN OAKS
"The Battle of Seven Oaks." Pierre Falcon. Translated by James Reaney. From *Poems*, by James Reaney. Victoria, B.C.: Press Porcépic, 1972; for permission to reprint, thanks are due to James Reaney and Press Porcépic.

6. THE REBELLION OF 1837
"Avant tout je suis Canadien." Sir George Etienne Cartier. John Boyd, *Sir George Etienne Cartier, Bart.* 1914.
" 'De Papineau Gun.' " William Henry Drummond. *Dr. Drummond's Complete Poems*. 1926.
"Un Canadien Errant." Antoine Gérin-Lajoie. *The Oxford Book of Canadian Verse in English and French*. 1960. Edited by A. J. M. Smith.

206

"Lord! Free Us All!" *Mackenzie's Gazette*,
November 3, 1838. Reprinted in *Rhymes of
Rebellion* (1965) edited by John S. Moir.

"National Anthem." *Montreal Transcript*,
February 13, 1838. Reprinted in *Rhymes of
Rebellion* (1965) edited by John S. Moir.

"Separate Inscriptions for the Graves
. . ." Raymond Souster. *Change Up*. Ottawa:
Oberon Press, 1974. Reprinted from *Collected Poems of Raymond Souster* by permission of Oberon Press.

7. THE FENIAN RAIDS

"The Fenian Blood-Hounds." W. Case.
Unpublished broadsheet, Baldwin Room,
Metropolitan Toronto Library. "Richmond
Hill, Sept. 10, 1866."

8. THE MOUNTED POLICE

"The Riders of the Plains." *Wake the Prairie Echoes*. 1973. Edited by the Saskatoon
History and Folklore Society.

9. THE RIEL REBELLIONS

"The Toronto Volunteers." *Singing Our
History*. Toronto: Doubleday, 1984. Edited
by Edith Fowke.

"The Man with the Gatling Gun."
Charles Pelham Mulvaney. *The History of
the North-West Rebellion of 1885*. 1886.

"The Charge at Batoche." J. W. Bengough. *Verses Grave and Gay*. 1895.

"The Battlefield at Batoche." Al Purdy.
Sex and Death. Toronto: McClelland and
Stewart, 1973. Used by permission of
McClelland and Stewart Limited, Toronto.

"Riel, 16 Novembre, 1885." Raymond
Souster. *As Is* 1967. Reprinted from *Collected Poems of Raymond Souster* by permission of Oberon Press.

"In Memoriam." Frederick George Scott.
Songs of the Great Dominion. 1889. Edited
by W. D. Lighthall.

10. THE NILE EXPEDITION

"The Canadians on the Nile." William
Wye Smith. *Songs of the Great Dominion*.
1889. Edited by W. D. Lighthall.

11. THE BOER WAR

"Kruger and the Boer War." Ebenezer
Bain. *Ramblings in Rhymeland*. 1918.

"On the Bust of an Army Corporal . . ."
Don Coles. *Anniversaries: Poems*. Toronto:
Macmillan, 1979. Reprinted by permission
of Macmillan of Canada.

12. THE FIRST WORLD WAR

"Wrong Turn at Sarajevo." Raymond
Souster. *Change Up*. Ottawa: Oberon Press,
1974. Reprinted from *Collected Poems of
Raymond Souster* by permission of Oberon
Press.

"We Are Coming, Mother Britain."
Wilfred Campbell. *The Poetical Works of
Wilfred Campbell*. 1922.

"We Are the Royal Highlanders." *Regimental Song Book*. Princess Patricia's Canadian Light Infantry, undated, early 1960s.

"The Easter Parade, 1915." R. S. Weir.
After Ypres and Other Verse. 1917.

"After the Speeches about the Empire."
Ted Plantos. *Passchendaele*. Windsor: Black
Moss Press, 1983. Reprinted by permission
of the publisher.

"Some Songs of the C.E.F." Unpublished
manuscript collection of World War I songs.

"It's a Long Way to Tipperary." Harry
H. Williams. Unpublished manuscript
version.

"Madelon." Alfred Bryant. Unpublished
manuscript version.

"Mademoiselle from Armentières." Gitz
Rice. Unpublished manuscript version.

"A Song of Winter Weather." Robert W.
Service. *Collected Poems*. New York: Dodd
Mead, 1964. Originally published in *The
Rhymes of a Red Cross Man*, 1916. Copy-
right by Dodd Mead. Used by permission,
Estate of Robert Service.

"Our Dug-Out." Edgar W. McInnis.
Poems Written at "The Front". (11th Canadian Siege Battery, Charlottetown, 1918).

"The Petrol Tin." W. J. Johnston. *The
Plain Speaker and Public Opinion*, October
1918. Reprinted in *The Poetry of the Canadian People*. 1976. Edited by N. Brian Davis.

"A Pot of Tea." Robert W. Service. *Col-
lected Poems*. New York: Dodd Mead, 1964.
Originally published in *The Rhymes of a Red
Cross Man*, 1916. Copyright by Dodd Mead.
Used by permission, Estate of Robert
Service.

"Ballad of Booze." Lieutenant Jack Turner. *Buddy's Blighty*. 1918.

"From the Trenches." J. R. Smith. *B.C. Federationist*, September 8, 1916. Reprinted in *The Poetry of the Canadian People*. 1976. Edited by N. Brian Davis.

"Keep Your Head Down, Fritzie Boy." Gitz Rice. Unpublished manuscript version.

"Of Lice and Silk." Ted Plantos. *Passchendaele*. Windsor: Black Moss Press, 1983. Reprinted by permission of the publisher.

"Brother Newt to Brother Fly." Philip Child. *God's Sparrows*. Toronto: McClelland and Stewart, 1937. The verse is identified as being "From Quentin's Notebook." Used by permission of McClelland and Stewart Limited, Toronto.

"Going Over." Charles G. D. Roberts. *New Poems*. 1919. Reprinted in *Canada Speaks of Britain* (1941), edited by Charles G. D. Roberts. Reprinted by permission of Lady Roberts.

"War." Arthur Stringer. *The Woman in the Rain and Other Poems*. 1907.

"I Didn't Raise My Boy to Be a Soldier." Alfred Bryant. Unpublished manuscript version.

"Cambrai and Marne." Charles G. D. Roberts. *Canada Speaks of Britain*. 1941. Edited by Charles G. D. Roberts. Reprinted by permission of Lady Roberts.

"Gas Clouds." Ted Plantos. *Passchendaele*. Windsor, Black Moss Press, 1983. Reprinted by permission of the publisher.

"The Third Battle of Ypres." Raymond Souster. *Place of Meeting*. 1967. Reprinted from *Collected Poems of Raymond Souster* by permission of Oberon Press.

"Ypres." Bruce Meyer. *Aurora: New Canadian Writing 1979*. 1979. Edited by Morris Wolfe. Reprinted by permission of the author.

"Ypres: 1915." Alden Nowlan. *The Mysterious Naked Man*. Toronto: Clarke, Irwin, 1969. © 1969 Clarke Irwin & Company Limited. Used by permission of Irwin Publishing Inc.

"Passchendaele, October 1917." Raymond Souster. *Collected Poems: Volume 4: 1974-1977*. Ottawa: Oberon Press, 1980. Reprinted from *Collected Poems of Raymond Souster* by permission of Oberon Press.

"To a Canadian Aviator . . ." Duncan Campbell Scott. *Selected Poems*. Toronto: McClelland and Stewart, 1947.

"The Avenging Angel." Wilfred Campbell. *The Poetical Works of Wilfred Campbell*. 1922.

"Our Women." L. M. Montgomery. *Canadian Poems of the Great War*. 1918. Edited by John W. Garvin.

"War Music: Rationing." Daisy Cook. Unpublished manuscript poem by a VAD nurse in World War I. Published by permission of the author.

"The Girl Behind the Man Behind the Gun." Wilson MacDonald. *Canadian Poets of the Great War*. 1918. Edited by John W. Garvin.

"K-K-K-Katy." Geoffrey O'Hara. Unpublished manuscript version of the song copyright in 1918 by Leo Feist.

"In Flanders Fields." John McCrae. *In Flanders Fields and Other Poems*. 1919. Edited by Sir Andrew Macphail.

"In Flanders Now." Edna Jaques. *Beside Still Waters*. Saskatoon: Western Producer Prairie Books, 1939.

"The Vimy Memorial." Watson Kirkconnell. *Centennial Tales and Selected Poems*. Toronto: University of Toronto Press, 1965.

"Vimy Unveiling." Joe Wallace. *Poems*. Toronto: Progress Books, 1981. Reprinted by permission of the publisher.

"Foye Buckner of Hainesville . . ." Alden Nowlan. *Bread, Wine and Salt*. Toronto: Clarke, Irwin, 1967. © Clarke Irwin & Company Limited. Used by permission of Irwin Publishing Inc.

"Two Canadian Memorials." Rudyard Kipling. *Verse: Definitive Edition*. 1940.

"Memorial Chamber Inscription." Rudyard Kipling. Inscription, Memorial Chamber, Peace Tower, Parliament Buildings, Ottawa.

13. THE SPANISH CIVIL WAR

"Battle Hymn of the Spanish Revolution." L. A. MacKay. *Viper's Bugloss*. 1938.

"To One Gone to the Wars." A. M. Klein. *The Canadian Forum*, June, 1938. Reprinted in *The Collected Poems of A. M. Klein*. Reprinted by permission of McGraw-Hill Ryerson Limited.

"Spain." Dorothy Livesay. *Collected Poems: The Two Seasons.* Toronto: McGraw-Hill Ryerson, 1972. Reprinted by permission of McGraw-Hill Ryerson Limited.

"Red Moon." Norman Bethune. *The Canadian Forum,* July 1937.

"I Come from Cuatro Caminos." Norman Bethune. Roderick Stewart, *The Mind of Norman Bethune.* Toronto: Fitzhenry & Whiteside, 1977.

"Our Morning Star." Joe Wallace. *Poems.* Toronto: Progress Books, 1981. Reprinted by permission of the publisher.

14. THE SECOND WORLD WAR
"Creed." Dick Diespecker. *Three Floors West.* Toronto: J. M. Dent, 1956.

ARMY
"In Time of War." Dorothy Livesay. *Collected Poems: The Two Seasons.* Toronto: McGraw-Hill Ryerson, 1972. Reprinted by permission of McGraw-Hill Ryerson Limited.

"On Going to the Wars." Earle Birney. *David and Other Poems.* 1942. Reprinted by permission of the author.

"The Second World War." Milton Acorn. *Dig Up My Heart.* Toronto: McClelland and Stewart, 1983. Used by permission of McClelland and Stewart Limited, Toronto.

"Recruit." Douglas Lochhead. *The Full Furnace.* Toronto: McGraw-Hill Ryerson, 1975. Reprinted by permission of the author.

"About Being a Member of Our Armed Forces." Al Purdy. *Being Alive.* Toronto: McClelland and Stewart, 1978. Used by permission of McClelland and Stewart Limited, Toronto.

"Canadian Women's Army Corps." *Athene: Goddess of War — The Canadian Women's Army Corps: Their Story* (1983) by W. Hugh Conrod.

"WAVE." Unpublished manuscript collection.

"Willie the Lion." Raymond Souster. *The Colour of the Times,* 1964. Reprinted from *Collected Poems of Raymond Souster* by permission of Oberon Press.

"Zombies." Unpublished manuscript collection.

"Letter Home." Unpublished manuscript collection.

"The Multipedes on the Road." E. J. Pratt. *Dunkirk* (excerpt), included in *The Collected Poems of E. J. Pratt.* Toronto: Macmillan, 1962. Reprinted by permission of University of Toronto Press.

"Wednesday, May 29." Robert Finch. *Dover Beach Revisited.* Toronto: Macmillan, 1961. Reprinted by permission of the agent for Robert Finch.

"Jubilee." Peter Taylor. *Trainer.* Sutton West: The Paget Press, 1980.

"Dieppe." George Whalley. *No Man An Island.* Toronto: Clarke, Irwin, 1948. © 1948 Clarke Irwin & Company Limited. Used by permission of Irwin Publishing Inc.

"This Was My Brother." Mona Gould. *Tasting the Earth.* Toronto: Macmillan, 1943. Reprinted by permission of the author and Gage Educational Publishing Company.

"Hong Kong, 1941." Raymond Souster. *Collected Poems: Volume 4: 1974–1977.* Ottawa: Oberon Press, 1980. Reprinted from *Collected Poems of Raymond Souster* by permission of Oberon Press.

"Sicilian Vignette." George Whalley. *No Man An Island.* Toronto: Clarke, Irwin, 1948. © 1948 Clarke Irwin & Company Limited. Used by permission of Irwin Publishing Inc.

"You'll Get Used to It." Freddy Grant. Eric Koch, *Deemed Suspect: A Wartime Blunder.* Toronto: Methuen, 1980.

"Three Verses from the Italian Front." *Rhyme and Reason.* Rome: Canadian Public Relations Services, February 1945.

"Meditation after an Engagement." Douglas LePan. *The Net and the Sword.* Toronto: Clarke, Irwin, 1953. Reprinted by permission of the author.

"Normandy 1944." George Whalley. *No Man An Island.* Toronto: Clarke, Irwin, 1948. © 1948 Clarke Irwin & Company Limited. Used by permission of Irwin Publishing Inc.

"One of the Regiment." Douglas LePan. *The Net and the Sword.* Toronto: Clarke,

Irwin, 1953. Reprinted by permission of the author.

"The Road to Nijmegen." Earle Birney. *The Collected Poems*. Toronto: McClelland and Stewart, 1975. Used by permission of McClelland and Stewart Limited, Toronto.

"Nijmegen, Holland, 1944." Raymond Souster. *Going the Distance*. Ottawa: Oberon Press, 1983. Reprinted from *Collected Poems of Raymond Souster* by permission of Oberon Press.

"Ex-Sergeant Whalen Tells the Story." Alden Nowlan. *Smoked Glass*. Toronto: Clarke, Irwin, 1977. © 1977 Clarke Irwin & Company Limited. Used by permission of Irwin Publishing Inc.

NAVY
"Royal Canadian Navy Volunteer Reserve." Unpublished manuscript collection.

"The Naval Control Service Officer. . . ." E. J. Pratt. *Behind the Log* (excerpt), included in *The Collected Poems*. Toronto: Macmillan, 1962. Reprinted by permission of University of Toronto Press.

"Gunboat Sortie." George Whalley. *No Man An Island*. Toronto: Clarke, Irwin, 1948. © 1948 Clarke Irwin & Company Limited. Used by permission of Irwin Publishing Inc.

"Memo from a Freighter." Dick Diespecker. *Three Floors West*. Toronto: J. M. Dent, 1956.

"The Fighting *P.R.*" George Dann's unpublished manuscript collection. Published by permission of the author.

"Sea Burial." George Whalley's *Battle Pattern* included in *No Man An Island*. Toronto: Clarke, Irwin, 1948. © 1948 Clarke Irwin & Company Limited. Used by permission of Irwin Publishing Inc.

AIR FORCE
"High Flight." John Gillespie Magee, Jr. *The New Treasury of War Poetry: Poems of the Second World War*. 1943. Edited by George Herbert Clarke.

"Watching Aircraft Take Off for Germany." Raymond Souster. *Collected Poems: Volume 4: 1974–1977*. Ottawa: Oberon Press, 1980. Reprinted from *Collected Poems of Raymond Souster* by permission of Oberon Press.

"Wartime Air Base." Al Purdy. *Sex and Death*. Toronto: McClelland and Stewart, 1973. Used by permission of McClelland and Stewart Limited, Toronto.

"The Heart to Carry On." Bertram Warr. *Acknowledgement to Life*. Toronto: Ryerson, 1970. Edited by Len Gasparini.

"Raid on the Ruhr, 1945." Raymond Souster. *Collected Poems: Volume 4, 1974–1977*. Ottawa: Oberon Press, 1980. Reprinted from *Collected Poems of Raymond Souster* by permission of Oberon Press.

"In Memory of James Eagleson, R.C.A.F." Douglas Lochhead. *The Full Furnace*. Toronto: McGraw-Hill Ryerson, 1975. Reprinted by permission of the author.

"Hymn for Those in the Air." Duncan Campbell Scott. *The Circle of Affection*. Toronto: McClelland and Stewart, 1947.

AFTERMATH
"May 8th, 1945." Roy Daniells. *The Chequered Shade*. Toronto: McClelland and Stewart, 1963.

"Remembering Esquimalt." Robin Skelton. *The Collected Shorter Poems*. Victoria: Sono Nis, 1981. Reprinted by permission of the author.

"Dedication." Ralph Gustafson. *Flight into Darkness*. 1944. Reprinted by permission of the author.

15. THE KOREAN WAR

"War on the Periphery." George Johnston. *The Cruising Auk*. 1959. Reprinted by permission; © 1951, 1979 The New Yorker Magazine, Inc.

"The Ric-a-Dam Doo." *Regimental Song Book*. Princess Patricia's Canadian Light Infantry, undated, early 1960s.

"Korean Saki." *Regimental Song Book*. Princess Patricia's Canadian Light Infantry, undated, early 1960s.

"Ghost Jumpers in the Sky." *Regimental Song Book*. Princess Patricia's Canadian Light Infantry, undated, early 1960s.

"Korea." Pat W. O'Connor. John Melady, *Korea: Canada's Forgotten War*. 1983.

16. PEACEKEEPING AND PROTEST

"Lest We Forget." F. R. Scott. *Overture.* 1945. From *Collected Poems.* Used by permission of McClelland and Stewart Limited, Toronto.

"Summer Will Come . . ." Joe Wallace. *Poems.* Toronto: Progress Books, 1981. Reprinted by permission of the publisher.

"Universal Soldier." Buffy Sainte-Marie. *The Buffy Sainte-Marie Songbook.* New York: Grosset & Dunlap, 1971. Edited by Peter Greenwood. Copyright © 1968 by Caleb Music. Reprinted by permission

"The Peaceable Kingdom." Al Purdy. *Sex and Death.* Toronto: McClelland and Stewart, 1973. Used by permission of McClelland and Stewart Limited, Toronto.

"On the Renewal of Bombing . . ." Eli Mandel. *Stony Plain.* Victoria: Press Porcépic, 1973. Reprinted by permission of Press Porcépic Limited.

"The Bronze Piper." Milton Acorn. *Dig Up My Heart.* Toronto: McClelland and Stewart, 1983. Used by permission of McClelland and Stewart Limited, Toronto.

17. FUTURE BATTLES

"World War III." Earle Birney. *The Collected Poems.* Toronto: McClelland and Stewart, 1975. Used by permission of McClelland and Stewart Limited, Toronto.